OCCASIONAL PAPER 251

The Design and Implementation of Deposit Insurance Systems

David S. Hoelscher, Michael Taylor, and Ulrich H. Klueh

INTERNATIONAL MONETARY FUND

Washington DC

2006

Production: IMF Multimedia Services Division
Typesetting: Bob Lunsford
Figures: Jason Soleil

Cataloging-in-Publication Data

Hoelscher, David S.
The design and implementation of deposit insurance systems / David S. Hoelscher, Michael Taylor, and Ulrich H. Klueh — [Washington, D.C. : International Monetary Fund, 2006]
    p. cm. — (Occasional paper ; 251)

    Includes bibliographical references.
    ISBN 1-58906-503-4

1. Deposit insurance. 2. Moral hazard. I. Taylor, Michael (Michael W.), 1962– II. Klueh, Ulrich. II. Series: Occasional paper (International Monetary Fund) ; no. 251
HG1662.A3H64 2006

Price: US$30.00
(US$28.00 to full-time faculty members and
students at universities and colleges)

Please send orders to:
International Monetary Fund, Publication Services
700 19th Street, N.W., Washington, D.C. 20431, U.S.A.
Tel.: (202) 623-7430   Telefax: (202) 623-7201
E-mail: publications@imf.org
Internet: http://www.imf.org

Contents

Figure

Boxes

Statistical Appendix Tables

The following conventions are used in this publication:

- In tables, a blank cell indicates "not applicable," ellipsis points (. . .) indicate "not available," and 0 or 0.0 indicates "zero" or "negligible." Minor discrepancies between sums of constituent figures and totals are due to rounding.

- An en dash (–) between years or months (for example, 2005–06 or January–June) indicates the years or months covered, including the beginning and ending years or months; a slash or virgule (/) between years or months (for example, 2005/06) indicates a fiscal or financial year, as does the abbreviation FY (for example, FY2006).

- "Billion" means a thousand million; "trillion" means a thousand billion.

- "Basis points" refer to hundredths of 1 percentage point (for example, 25 basis points are equivalent to ¼ of 1 percentage point).

As used in this publication, the term "country" does not in all cases refer to a territorial entity that is a state as understood by international law and practice. As used here, the term also covers some territorial entities that are not states but for which statistical data are maintained on a separate and independent basis.

Preface

Countries are modifying their deposit insurance systems at a rapid pace as lessons are learned about the possible limitations of deposit insurance and the effectiveness of design features. Considerable changes were introduced by the transition economies in Central and Eastern Europe in the early and mid-1990s. Lessons from that experience were summarized in a number of IMF publications surveying country practices, which were shared with the membership at large.[1] By the mid- and late 1990s, a significant number of countries had introduced deposit protection systems as a means of stabilizing their banking systems and protecting depositors from loss. The IMF assisted in the design of such systems but cautioned about too rapid an introduction, suggesting that appropriate political, institutional, and economic preconditions needed to be in place before deposit protection could be effective. By 2000, the IMF reviewed this experience and identified "good international practices" that were emerging from the country experience.[2]

Together with the rapid growth in the number of deposit insurance systems, academic papers raised a series of concerns about the appropriate design of safety nets in general and deposit insurance systems in particular. Issues concerned the incentive structures of deposit insurance systems and the possibility of linkages between deposit insurance design and financial sector vulnerabilities.

This paper reviews recent developments in the design of deposit insurance systems and offers a summary of the academic literature. As in the past, the IMF's work on deposit insurance argues against the development of "best practices" applicable to all systems but, rather, stresses the importance of incorporating the authorities' objectives as well as individual country characteristics when adopting a deposit insurance system to ensure an effective system that minimizes disincentives and distortions to financial sector intermediation.

The authors would like to thank David Parker for his substantial assistance in discussing the design issues and in preparing the text. They would also like to thank members of the European Forum, the International Association of Deposit Insurers, and the World Bank for insightful comments. Administrative assistants Sandra Solares and Aster Teklemariam provided excellent support. The text has also benefited from the editorial expertise of Marina Primorac and Jeffrey Hayden from the External Relations Department, who coordinated its publication.

---

[1]Kyei (1995) and Garcia (1996).
[2]Garcia (2000).

Abbreviations

ALL	Allowance for loan losses
CAMELS	Capital, Asset Quality, Management, Earnings, Liquidity, and Sensitivity (credit worthiness assessment system)
CAR	Capital adequacy ratio
CD	Certificate of deposit
CDIC	Canada Deposit Insurance Corporation
CEO	Chief Executive Officer
DIA	Deposit insurance agency
DIS	Deposit insurance system
DPB	Deposit Protection Board (Zimbabwe)
EEA	European Economic Area
EU	European Union
FDIC	Federal Deposit Insurance Agency
FGD	Fondo de Garantia de Depositos (Paraguay)
FOGADE	Fondo de Garantia de Depositos de las Instituciones Financieras
FOSEDE	Fondo de Seguro de Depositos
FSA	Financial Services Authority (United Kingdom)
FSF	Financial Stability Forum
IADI	International Association of Deposit Insurers
IDIC	Indonesian Deposit Insurance Corporation
MOF	Ministry of Finance
MOU	Memorandum of Understanding
OECD	Organization for Economic Cooperation and Development

I Overview

Deposit insurance systems have developed and expanded rapidly in recent years. A large number of countries have modified their systems, either adopting explicit deposit insurance systems or introducing significant modifications to existing systems. In addition, the international community has participated in the debate on the appropriate design of safety nets in general and deposit insurance in particular. In 2001, a working group of the Financial Stability Forum (FSF) published a report on the broad range of options for establishing a deposit insurance system. In 2003, the International Association of Deposit Insurers (IADI) was established to promote international cooperation and to encourage widespread international contact among deposit insurers.

In light of these recent developments, this paper has two broad objectives. First, recently established insurance systems are described, identifying emerging trends. A number of studies have surveyed deposit insurance practices. Two previous IMF publications (Garcia, 1996, 2000) remain valuable references as do the surveys conducted by the IADI in 2002 and 2003 on 47 countries.[1] This paper updates those surveys.[2] It is based on public information obtained from central banks, ministries of finance, and deposit insurance agencies and on the 2003 update of the World Bank's database on banking regulation.

The second objective of this paper is to identify sound practices in deposit insurance based on recent experience. The starting point is the FSF report (FSF, 2001) containing over 40 recommendations, ranging from broad policy considerations to detailed directions on the management and operation of a deposit insurance system. The paper builds on that guidance, identifies good practices in the design of deposit insurance systems, and provides evidence for resolving the trade-offs identified by the FSF.

This paper also seeks to place these policy recommendations within the growing body of economic literature on deposit insurance systems. Recent years have seen a number of attempts to develop econometric tests of the influence exercised by explicit deposit insurance, as well as the impact of different design features of deposit insurance systems. This work requires careful consideration, not least because some of it has been used to draw policy conclusions about the merits of adopting explicit deposit insurance. A number of these studies conclude that the existence of explicit systems increases the risk of banking crises, and also points to design features—such as the desirability of ex post funding—that run counter to the views of many deposit insurance practitioners.

The sound practices described in this paper are not meant to become "best practices" or "core principles" such as those developed by international standard setters.[3] Rather, they are meant to outline international experience in resolving the most important issues related to deposit insurance alternatives, illustrating that some design features can be seen as comparatively more efficient than others. Authorities may well opt for practices different from those described here, reflecting concerns about local conditions or specialized objectives. The description of the procedures contained here is not meant to change such decisions. Rather, the paper seeks to ensure that relevant factors are taken into consideration as such decisions are made.

The structure of this paper is as follows. Section II includes a discussion of explicit and implicit deposit insurance, including recent academic literature and policy recommendations. Section III reviews the conditions to be weighed when considering the introduction of a deposit insurance system, including policy objectives and necessary preconditions. Section IV provides specific design features of deposit insurance systems, including mandates, powers, accountability, transparency, funding, membership, cover, and public awareness. Section V discusses design features aimed at minimizing the impact of moral hazard.

---

[1]The completed questionnaires as well as a brief summary of findings are available at www.iadi.org.

[2]Approximately 200 countries have been included and updated in the survey.

[3]For example, the Basel Committee developed the Basel Core Principles for Effective Banking Supervision, and both the Organization of Economic Cooperation and Development and the International Association of Insurance Supervisors have developed core principles for the supervision and regulation of securities markets and insurance companies, respectively.

II Explicit and Implicit Deposit Insurance

The Choice between Explicit and Implicit Deposit Insurance

Sound Practice: Explicit deposit insurance has a number of important advantages compared with implicit insurance.

Policymakers have a variety of options concerning the protection of depositors. Countries can make explicit the protection of depositors in the case of a bank failure or they can leave the level of protection ambiguous, allowing the level and coverage of depositor protection implicit. Explicit protection lays out the level and the limits that depositors can expect in case of a bank failure, whereas implicit protection systems allow the conditions and limits to be negotiated during the failure process.

An explicit deposit insurance system is rules-based, clarifying the government's obligations to protect depositors when a bank is unable to meet its repayment obligations. An explicit deposit insurance system is expressly laid down by statute or other legal instrument, and there are rules concerning compensation limits, the types of obligations covered, the methods for calculating obligations, funding arrangements, and other matters. An explicit deposit insurance system clarifies the financial obligations of the banking system and the public sector. For this reason, an explicit system restricts the extent of subjective or ad hoc decisions.

Some authorities have opted for a system of depositor preference instead of an explicit deposit insurance system. Under this arrangement depositors are given priority over other unsecured creditors in the distribution of proceeds from liquidation of a failed bank. Although this improves the depositors' position in cases of bank insolvency, the bank's assets may nonetheless still be insufficient to meet their claims in full, and depositors may also face long delays in receiving their funds.[4]

Where explicit deposit insurance systems do not exist, implicit deposit insurance is a pervasive feature of bank safety nets. The main characteristics of implicit deposit insurance include the absence of any rules regarding the coverage or compensation for losses and the absence of funds available for assistance. As a result, decisions on depositor protection are negotiated at the time of a bank failure. Possibilities exist for inconsistent treatment of depositors and other creditors, mixed market signals concerning the intentions of the authorities, and the reliance on discretionary government funding for bank failures (Kyei, 1995). Although implicit systems provide considerable flexibility for the authorities and allow "constructive ambiguity," thus reducing the moral hazard that exists in any insurance system, the costs of such flexibility in terms of system efficiency and the resolution costs of crises must be carefully considered.

Some countries have tried to make an unambiguous commitment to offering neither explicit nor implicit deposit insurance. The clearest recent example is New Zealand, which takes a distinctive approach to banking supervision and does not offer deposit insurance. Such a policy may be feasible under some circumstances—for example, when the banking system is almost exclusively owned by strong foreign institutions (see discussion in Section IV). However, it is difficult to sustain over periods of economic and financial distress. A prominent example is Argentina, which between 1991 and 1995 abolished deposit insurance and announced a clear and unambiguous commitment to not protecting depositors. This policy was abandoned during the 1995 Tequila Crisis, when concerns about depositor reaction in the face of the deep financial difficulties led the authorities to reverse their stand and reinstate deposit insurance.

Moral Hazard

Sound Practice: When combined with other factors, such as effective regulation and supervision, specific design features of the deposit insurance system can reduce moral hazard.

A discussion of explicit deposit insurance must address moral hazard, which in this context is defined as "... the incentive for excessive risk taking by banks or those receiving the benefit of (deposit insurance) protection" (FSF, 2001). As in any insurance system, a deposit insurance system can lead to moral hazard in the form of excessive risk taking by institutions with insured liabilities. Although moral hazard cannot be

---

[4]This has been a factor in Hong Kong SAR's decision to switch from a system of depositor priority to explicit limited deposit insurance.

eliminated, the safety net can be designed to reduce the distortions introduced by moral hazard considerations. Clarity on the responsibilities of bank shareholders and strong supervision with early intervention capacity are good examples. In addition, specific design features of the deposit insurance system can be introduced to limit moral hazard, including coinsurance, risk-based insurance premiums, and mandatory subordinated debt issuance, among others. The appropriate system will depend on the specific institutional environment within which the deposit insurance system operates. Section V provides a detailed discussion on this issue.

Recent Academic Literature on Explicit Deposit Insurance

In recent years a number of econometric studies have attempted to evaluate the economic consequences of introducing explicit deposit insurance. Some of these studies suggest a statistical correlation between an explicit deposit insurance scheme and the increased risk of a systemic crisis. The paper by Demirgüç-Kunt and Kane (2002) may be taken as representative of this literature. Building on the results of Demirgüç-Kunt and Detragiache (2002), Demirgüç-Kunt and Kane (2002) argue that increased risk taking owing to an explicit deposit insurance system manifests itself in an increased probability of experiencing a systemic crisis.

Although a strong institutional environment—indicated by measures of bureaucratic quality, lack of corruption, contract enforcement, and legal efficiency interacted with deposit insurance variables—mitigates the effects to a certain degree (interaction terms are negative and significant), explicit deposit insurance still significantly increases bank fragility. Thus Demirgüç-Kunt and Kane (2002) question the desirability of an explicit deposit insurance system and claim that "officials in many countries should close their ears to the siren call of explicit deposit insurance" (p. 192). Even though the authors point out that the research summarized in their paper "by no means implies that all countries with explicit systems should close them down at the first opportunity," several of their findings (for example, concerning the desirability of ex post systems) stand in sharp contrast to earlier assessments of good practice and deposit insurance design (see Garcia, 2000).

A number of econometric studies have raised questions about the robustness of the Demirgüç-Kunt and Kane (2002) conclusions.[5] Although Demirgüç-Kunt and

Kane (2002) perform various robustness tests, the conclusion that explicit deposit insurance increases the risk of systemic crisis is not replicated in other binary models of banking crises. For instance, Eichengreen and Arteta (2000), in an attempt to consolidate recent work on the determinants of banking crises, find that the effect of explicit systems is highly sensitive to the use of different crisis lists and deposit insurance series, and to the exclusion of several types of countries. A particularly striking feature is that the exclusion of Organization for Economic Cooperation and Development (OECD) countries weakens the effect of deposit insurance on crisis probability, since OECD countries are expected to have a contract environment favorable to a deposit insurance system.[6] The authors conclude that "there is at least as much evidence that deposit insurance has favorable effects . . . as that it destabilizes banking systems. . . ." (p. 25).

Moreover, the theoretical basis for the proposition that explicit deposit insurance increases banking fragility needs to be carefully reviewed. Demirgüç-Kunt and Kane (2002) argue that an explicit scheme will be detrimental to private monitoring efforts, thus weakening market discipline. However, the proposition that in the absence of deposit insurance, small-scale depositors will effectively monitor banks is less than obvious. Specifically, as argued by Dewatripont and Tirole (1994), small-scale depositors are often uninformed and suffer from a coordination problem, thus lacking the incentives to acquire the necessary information to discipline banks effectively. A solution to the coordination problem is for them to be represented by an agent that intervenes contingent on the bank's performance. According to this theory, the additional effect of making depositor claims less secure should be marginal. Hence, it would be far more important to involve large creditors in efforts to effectively control risk taking, one of the central objectives of an explicit limited deposit insurance system.

Critics of deposit insurance contend that the introduction of an explicit deposit insurance system will hamper market discipline, because covered depositors will lose their incentives to discipline banks. Most of the studies cited to underpin this line of reasoning use data from the United States (Flannery, 1998, provides an extensive survey of the relevant literature), a country with a relatively high coverage level relative to GDP and with a highly developed financial system. As a consequence, it is not clear whether the results carry over to other environments, although the work by Demirgüç-Kunt and Huizinga (2004) suggests that similar effects may be found elsewhere. These authors use a sample of up to 2,500 banks in 43 countries to examine how bank characteristics influence the interest cost and the growth rate of deposits for banks operating in countries with or without

---

[5]Robustness tests include a two-stage procedure to control for the possibility that countries with weak banking systems are more likely to introduce a deposit insurance system, the use of a principal component measure of moral hazard instead of the deposit insurance characteristics, and the inclusion of other variables characterizing the banking system.

[6]Note that this result depends on the way explanatory variables are weighted to account for measurement errors.

an explicit deposit insurance system. They find that an explicit scheme indeed lowers the sensitivity of banks' interest rate expenses to changes in risk profiles.

Nonetheless, other econometric studies reach the opposite conclusion. Martinez Peria and Schmukler (2001) find that depositors in Argentina, Chile, and Mexico intensively disciplined banks during the 1980s and 1990s, and that deposit insurance did not significantly diminish the extent of market discipline. Gropp and Vesala (2004) conclude on the basis of a sample of 128 banks in 15 European countries that introducing explicit deposit insurance actually reduced risk taking. The authors argue that, by introducing explicit limits on coverage, European authorities were able to effectively reduce the expected public subsidy in case of failures.[7] The authors also find that certain bank characteristics produce different effects on risk-taking behavior when a deposit insurance system is introduced. Institutions having lower charter values and a higher share of subordinated debt reinforce the risk-mitigating effect of explicitly reducing coverage, whereas very large banks do not change their policies in reaction to deposit insurance. This latter result points to the importance of an integrated approach to the safety net and the way it shapes incentives.

In summary, recent econometric studies do not point to a firm conclusion regarding the effectiveness of private monitoring and the consequences of explicit deposit insurance systems on banks' risk-taking incentives. Depositors seem to respond rationally to bank performance in most circumstances, in particular when they are not covered by a deposit insurance system, but explicit systems do not have an impact on banks' risk taking that can be universally observed. In addition, an explicit deposit insurance scheme is only one component in a comprehensive bank safety net. Although the existence of a safety net will, on average, influence agents' risk-taking incentives, it is less clear that explicit deposit insurance will do so in a well-defined way that permits its influence to be distinguished from that of other financial safety elements.

---

[7]They acknowledge, however, that the observed effect might be partially due to other factors, including the role of European Union policy on state aids in discouraging bailout policies in member countries, and the fact that some countries that had introduced deposit insurance in the period under study had experienced a systemic crisis shortly before, causing authorities and depositors to be especially vigilant.

Policy Implications

The primary contrast between implicit and explicit deposit insurance systems is between discretion and rules. An implicit guarantee will allow the government to employ a strategy of constructive ambiguity and flexibility—for example, the extent to which depositors and shareholders receive a haircut can be made dependent on the availability of funds and/or the economic—and political—importance of the groups being affected by a bank failure. Thus, constructive ambiguity has the potential to increase private monitoring efforts but entails the danger of excessively discretionary policies, favoring those groups that are best organized to defend their interests. An implicit system may thus subject depositors to unplanned decisions under crisis conditions and result in unequal treatment of deposits, while at the same time maximizing the government's potential liability. To the extent that both large and small depositors and other classes of creditors may believe themselves to be protected by implicit insurance, market discipline will be reduced and moral hazard will be increased.

The introduction of an explicit scheme does not completely eliminate the potential for ad hoc decision making, but it does reduce its scope, provided that the scheme is credible. The potential for explicit deposit insurance to give rise to a problem of dynamic inconsistency is nonetheless real, and governments may still be tempted to override a rules-based system on political grounds or on the belief that institutions are either "too big" or "too many" to fail. In these situations, constructive ambiguity can be a positive thing, because although some banks may be "too big to fail," they are not given a competitive advantage by being explicitly designated as such.

Nonetheless, these issues potentially arise in all rules-based systems. The primary advantage of explicit deposit insurance is that it provides a mechanism to deal with depositors' claims equitably and transparently while limiting the government's potential liability. It is important to note that proponents of making the safety net explicit do not claim that depositors' incentives will be unaffected. They rather argue that the benefits of preventing bank runs outweigh the costs in terms of weaker market discipline, if and only if the loss of some market discipline can be augmented by appropriate regulation and supervision.

III   Introduction of a Deposit Insurance Scheme

Objectives

Sound Practice: The authorities should have clear and realistic objectives in establishing a deposit insurance scheme.

A deposit insurance system generally has two separate but complementary objectives within the overall framework of the financial safety net. The first is to contribute to the stability of the financial system as an adjunct to the central bank's lender of last resort function. The second is to provide a minimum level of protection to the wealth of the average household in the event of a bank failure.

Preservation of the Stability of the Financial System

The financial stability function of deposit insurance has been formally modeled by Diamond and Dybvig (1983). According to their model, the nature of the deposit contract gives an incentive for bank runs to develop, even if a bank is solvent. This is because of the "first come, first served" basis on which depositors' demand for liquidity is met. Until the bank declares closure it must meet deposit withdrawals on demand. Once its liquid assets and capacity to borrow liquidity (assumed to be equal to its capital) are exhausted, the bank is likely to be insolvent owing to the need to dispose of illiquid assets at distress prices. After closure, depositors join a pool of creditors who may or may not be repaid in full. Therefore, depositors carry a strong incentive to be first in the queue, and the risk that others may withdraw can cause a panic regardless of the underlying financial position of the bank. Deposit runs on banks thus arise as the result of a coordination problem among depositors. If all depositors try to redeem their deposits at the same time, a bank will fail. Deposit insurance ensures that depositors' funds will be protected from the risks and uncertainties of the normal liquidation process. By guaranteeing that individual depositors will be able to recover their money no matter what happens to the bank, deposit insurance removes the incentive to be first in the queue at the first sign of trouble. Thus, deposit insurance stabilizes banks by removing the incentives for bank runs to develop.

This role of deposit insurance can be thought of as a supplement to the lender of last resort function. The banking system benefits from the enhanced public confidence in the soundness of the financial system arising from a credible and well-designed deposit insurance system. The public-good character of confidence in the financial system justifies the element of cross-subsidy from stronger to weaker institutions that inevitably exist even in a well-designed scheme.

Compensation of Depositors

A second function of deposit insurance is to compensate small-scale depositors in the event that the institution fails. Deposit insurance is useful because the average depositor is not expected to have the skills or resources necessary to monitor bank activities.[8] An additional consideration is that the wealth of an average household, or one of below-average means, will often be poorly diversified. The typical household will usually own relatively few financial assets and have its financial wealth concentrated in basic deposit accounts at one or two institutions. A bank failure could inflict significant hardship. The purpose of deposit insurance may be described as insuring the financial wealth of the typical household and providing it with access to a safe means of making payments. In this sense it is no different than any other form of insurance. Compared with typical bankruptcy law, deposit insurance guarantees that depositors will receive at least a minimum amount of their deposit, irrespective of the quality of the bank's assets available for liquidation. In addition, the deposit insurance system could be designed to ensure that depositors receive their funds more quickly than would normally be the case under general bankruptcy law.

Although these objectives are not mutually exclusive, the relative weighting given to them can have important implications for the design features and modalities of the deposit insurance system. Hence the authorities need to be clear about which of the two objectives they wish to emphasize most in establishing a deposit insurance system. The financial stability objective points to the system's relatively broad membership (including deposit-taking institutions other than commercial banks) and to relatively generous coverage limits, with the caveat that if limits are set too high, risk taking could be encour-

---

[8]This rationale is also often applied to the existence of bank supervision and regulation more generally (Dewatripont and Tirole, 1994).

aged, thereby endangering stability. By contrast, a deposit insurance system that exists primarily to protect small-scale depositors will tend to have a relatively more limited membership (confined to institutions that primarily take "retail" deposits, however defined) and will have less generous coverage limits. Once the design is completed, the public must be made aware of the scope and purpose of the deposit insurance system.

Conditions for Effective Deposit Insurance

Sound Practice: The advantages of an explicit, limited deposit insurance system can best be realized if certain conditions are in place before its introduction.

A hierarchy of factors can be identified that affect the effectiveness of an explicit limited deposit insurance system, ranking them from the most critical to less critical. The most important factor is the existence of macroeconomic stability, followed closely by the soundness of the financial system. High standards of supervision and regulation are also important to limit the potential risk exposure of the deposit insurance system. Finally, the structure of the banking system also needs to be considered because it is relevant to the viability of the particular form of deposit insurance system under consideration. Thus the conditions under which countries should seek to move from implicit to explicit deposit insurance will be the product of a matrix of several factors.[9]

The most important of these factors relate to the condition of the macroeconomy and the soundness of the banking system. If the macroeconomic environment is unstable or the banking system is unsound there is a risk that a newly introduced deposit insurance system will fail. A deposit insurance system that is confronted by a wave of bank failures, or even the failure of a single very large bank, soon after it has been established, is likely to lack the resources to meet the resulting claims from depositors. It must either fail in its obligations to them or depend on government fiscal support. Either scenario severely damages the system's credibility and can lead to a loss of public confidence in the deposit insurance system. Once confidence has been lost, experience shows that it is extremely difficult to regain. Moreover, a loss of public confidence in the deposit insurance system could lead to a broader loss of confidence in the financial system, compounding the fragilities that had led to the initial round of bank fail-

ures. A deposit insurance system that is poorly implemented without the necessary preconditions being in place may thus trigger the very instability it had been established to prevent.

In considering the economic and institutional conditions and their impact on the options available for a deposit insurance system, some level of subjectivity is inevitable. For example, as described below, the boundary between "acceptable" and "unacceptable" macroeconomic conditions (such as inflation) or between concentrated and diversified industry structures are difficult to determine a priori. Rather, country-specific, historical factors and public sensitivity to the issues must be considered. For example, what may be an acceptable and "nondistortionary" inflation level in one country may not be acceptable in another.

The implication of the above is that the authorities can use the hierarchy outlined in this paper to guide their deliberations about the appropriate structure of deposit insurance systems and to identify options. But the actual decisions about which alternative to adopt must be clearly and firmly grounded in the experience and conditions in the country itself.

Macroeconomic Considerations

It is difficult for banks to conduct normal financial intermediation under conditions of macroeconomic instability, such as high inflation, a rapidly depreciating exchange rate, and/or collapsing economic growth. In these circumstances, it is difficult, if not impossible, for banks to judge adequately risks and, consequently, they cannot make proper lending decisions. Depositors and other creditors cannot differentiate between safe and unsafe banking practices and therefore cannot impose market discipline. In such cases, private sector confidence in the banking system deteriorates and financial intermediation can collapse.

Under conditions of macroeconomic instability, a limited deposit insurance system has a small role to play. The loss in private sector confidence results from the overall policy stance of the government, rather than from concern about the condition of the banking system. Introduction of a deposit insurance system to protect depositors cannot, by itself, address the causes of the macroeconomic deterioration. In other words, a deposit insurance system may be useful in preventing a banking crisis but only in a supportive macroeconomic environment, and it cannot cure a crisis that has already begun. For these reasons, introduction of a deposit insurance system under conditions of macroeconomic instability is considered inappropriate.

Condition of the Banking System

A number of factors related to the structure and financial conditions of a country's banking system can

---

[9]A further important precondition concerns the strength of the legal framework within which the deposit insurance agency will operate, and in particular the effectiveness of the insolvency regime for banks. Where the general law on insolvency is perceived to be ineffective, a possible solution is to provide for a special scheme for bank insolvency.

influence the design and implementation of a deposit insurance system.

Market-Based Banking System

In addition to macroeconomic conditions, an important consideration is whether financial intermediation is market based or is predominantly determined by the state. This issue is not primarily the ownership of the banking system, but rather the rules of the game governing financial intermediation. When planning a deposit insurance system, the banking system should operate according to market rules. Where the state makes the credit and investment decisions, rather than permitting the banking system to respond to market forces, it would not be credible to claim that the state does not stand behind the obligations of the banking system. Thus, even under conditions of macroeconomic stability, banking systems based on government-determined resource intermediation may not benefit from a deposit insurance system. Deposits are already perceived as having full guarantee, and the state must provide the resources to compensate depositors in the case of bank failure. Similarly, coverage restrictions are not meaningful. Partial coverage of a deposit insurance system is aimed at providing an incentive to depositors and other creditors to apply market discipline, moving their resources from banks following unsound banking practices to those following sound practices. When the state makes all operating decisions concerning financial intermediation, there is no competition and no alternative.

Similar considerations apply where, although some parts of the banking system may be in private ownership, the publicly owned banks dominate the system. This is the case, for example, in transition economies where the traditional dominance of the state savings bank in the retail deposit market has yet to be challenged by private institutions. As long as the deposit market is distorted by the existence of an institution that enjoys extensive, albeit implicit, government guarantees, there is limited scope for deposit insurance to redress the balance. Thus the introduction of a competitive deposit market and the reduction of the dominance of public banks can be regarded as important conditions for the successful introductions of a credible deposit insurance system.

Soundness of the Banking System

If the macroeconomic situation is sufficiently stable and the banking system is market based, another consideration is the soundness of the banking system. The question is not whether there are unsound banks in the banking system, but rather whether the banking system itself is facing a possible collapse because the number of banks in distress is large. In other words, is the banking system in need of fundamental restructuring?

A critical objective of a deposit insurance system is the strengthening of private sector confidence. That objective will be difficult to achieve if the system is not sound. Moreover, implementation of a deposit insurance system in an unsound banking system would reduce or remove incentives for depositors to exercise discipline, because unsound banks would be able to attract household deposits by offering high interest rates under the protection of the deposit insurance system. Depositors would have no incentive to police the banks and move deposits to safer banks. For the same reason, banks have no incentives *not* to engage in unsafe and unsound practices. In such circumstances, banks can remain insolvent but liquid, increasing the eventual costs of banking system restructuring.

Adequacy of Regulation and Legal Framework

If macroeconomic conditions are relatively stable—the banking system is both market based and sound—consideration should be given to the degree and effectiveness of banking supervision and regulation. Adequate prudential regulations and the legal framework for enforcing these regulations allow the authorities to set and enforce limits on risk taking by banks. Effective supervision and regulation is essential to ensure stability by limiting the amount of risk incurred by banks to acceptable levels. An adequate regulatory and legal framework therefore has the effect of counteracting the weakening of market discipline engendered by the existence of a bank safety net (of which deposit insurance is part) and reducing to a minimum the cost of the overall bank safety net.

Where prudential supervision and the enforcement of rules are weak, there is a risk that an explicit deposit insurance scheme may not be effective. Problems could arise in the misuse of deposit insurance system resources or in excessive risk taking owing to moral hazard. In the absence of an adequate regulatory infrastructure, the authorities would have little means of monitoring banking activity or limiting its risk taking, and the deposit insurer would face significant contingent liabilities. The frequent coincidence in the banking sector of poor regulation and enforcement practices with financial sector weaknesses further supports the need to consider the introduction of explicit deposit insurance as part of a proper sequencing of institutional development.

Closely connected to the importance of an adequate regulatory and supervisory infrastructure is the need for adequate bank resolution and insolvency policies. The banking system can be kept healthy only if weak and insolvent institutions are rapidly resolved. If they are permitted to continue to operate, they will increase long-term resolution costs and weaken otherwise healthy banks—for example, by bidding deposits away from them.

Banking System Structure

If the macroeconomic situation is stable, the financial sector is relatively sound and intermediation is governed by market forces, and supervision and regulation are adequate, then the final factor to be considered is the structure of the banking industry. Among the issues that arise is a high degree of banking system concentration, thus resulting in a few "too big to fail" institutions and the preponderance of foreign-owned institutions in the banking system.

System Concentration

A highly concentrated banking system—in which a few very large banks account for most financial intermediation—would require substantial resources to compensate depositors in the event that any of these banks should fail. Moreover, in a highly concentrated system it is more likely that any individual bank will be judged too big to fail and hence the authorities will commit public funds to ensure that it remains able to meet its financial obligations. This raises the question of whether a deposit insurance system can perform a useful function in a system with this structure.

Some countries with a highly concentrated banking system have opted not to offer deposit insurance. If the system contains a number of too big to fail institutions, it is argued that taxpayers will inevitably need to be called on to provide resources to resolve any serious problems, and hence an implicit, discretionary scheme has been preferred to an explicit, rules-based one. Examples of countries adopting this option include Australia and (until recently) Hong Kong SAR. Other countries with highly concentrated systems, such as Germany and the United Kingdom, have relied on privately funded mutual guarantees among the large banks in the system. The banks understand each other's business and can be in a better position to exert market discipline on one another. In such cases, deposit protection is provided ex post, thus increasing the incentives for banks to monitor each other and impose market discipline on each other.

However, very few banking systems are so highly concentrated that deposit insurance cannot play a useful role in promoting financial stability or in protecting the savings of small-scale depositors. Notwithstanding the existence of too-big-to-fail institutions, the failure of other banks in the system can raise financial stability issues, because experience suggests that contagion from the failure of a small bank can rapidly spread to other banks in the system, even to the large banks. To the extent that deposit insurance reduces the incentives for depositors to run from small banks, it thus can contribute to the stability of the system overall. Moreover, by introducing a deposit insurance system, the resolution of smaller banks is facilitated when necessary, whereas it is implicitly accepted that the deposit insurance system resources would need to be supplemented by public funds in the event that a large bank were to encounter difficulties. Thus the existence of the deposit insurance system can go some way toward passing the cost of dealing with bank failures on to the banking system itself, although it cannot do so entirely. This has been the arrangement adopted, for example, in Canada and the United Kingdom, and now in Hong Kong SAR.

Foreign Ownership

It is sometimes suggested that a high degree of foreign ownership in the banking system obviates the need for a deposit insurance system altogether. As discussed earlier, New Zealand provides the clearest example of this policy. There are, however, reasons for introducing a deposit insurance system even when a clear preponderance of banking system assets and liabilities are under the control of foreign banks (see Section IV on Membership). A foreign bank parent may fail to support its local subsidiary, or the parent bank itself may fail. In the event of the failure of the foreign parent, the laws of its home country may restrict the availability of assets to meet the claims of depositors overseas. Even if local subsidiary assets are available, there may be some delay in compensating depositors. Each of these factors means that there are risks in relying on the support of foreign banks for their local operations as a substitute for a deposit insurance scheme.

Whether the role of foreign banks in the financial system negates the effectiveness of a deposit insurance system has to be decided on a case-by-case basis. There may be a case for not implementing a deposit insurance scheme, if all the following conditions are met:
- the great preponderance of banking system liabilities are placed with foreign-owned banks;
- the foreign banks themselves are of impeccable reputation; and
- the foreign parent banks' home country authorities have both the capacity to support the parent banks (including ample foreign currency reserves) and the ability to subject them to full and comprehensive consolidated supervision.

For many countries, however, the foreign banks' penetration of their domestic financial systems will not dominate locally incorporated banks' share of liabilities. Moreover, especially in emerging market economies, the foreign banks might not be restricted to major international banks. There could also be foreign banks licensed by other emerging market countries that could lack the resources to adequately support cross-border operations. Thus, for most countries, foreign banks cannot realistically substitute for a deposit insurance system. If a deposit insurance system is established, then the foreign banks in the system should be required to become members (see Section IV on Membership).

IV Specific Design Features of Deposit Insurance Systems

The sound practices explained in this section are not designated as "best practices," but merely reflect international experience regarding the more important deposit insurance issues (Box 1). Although some design features described here have proven to be relatively more efficient and cost effective than others, the authorities may opt for different practices, depending on local conditions or specialized objectives.

A survey was conducted of 85 different systems of deposit protection that offer an explicit, limited deposit insurance system in normal times (Table 1). As the table shows, 6 of the surveyed countries are in Africa; 14 in Asia; 40 in Europe; 6 in the Middle East; and 19 in the Americas. The results of the survey are reviewed in this section.

Following are examples of specific design features that should be explicitly included in the deposit insurance law or regulation.

Mandates and Powers

Sound Practice: A deposit insurance agency's legal powers and human and financial resources should be appropriate to its mandate, and its actions should be well coordinated with those of other safety net players.

Every well-designed financial safety net will include several functions, namely, the lender of last resort, other forms of financial assistance (for example, solvency support provided by the fiscal authority), supervision and regulation, intervention and bank resolution powers, and deposit insurance. The distribution of these functions among institutions is a matter of public policy choice and will reflect the history, constitutional arrangements, and traditions of each country. For example, in some countries the central bank, as lender of last resort, is also the banking supervisor, whereas in other countries, the functions are separate. In addition, in some countries, the central bank also administers the deposit insurance fund. In other countries, each of these functions is administered by separate and autonomous institutions. Irrespective of the precise institutional form selected, the primary consideration is that the functions should be well coordinated and the system should be free of gaps.

Options for Institutional Structure

There are a range of options for structuring deposit insurance arrangements: the deposit insurance agency might operate autonomously or under the control of another institution (for example, the central bank or bank regulatory agency); and it also might have a range of powers, from a simple paybox structure to a "risk-minimizer," with a number of possibilities in between. These two issues—the extent of the agency's powers and the extent of its autonomy—are in reality closely connected.

The deposit insurance agency may be established as a simple "paybox" with the mandate to make compensation payouts to depositors. Where the agency is established as a paybox, it needs only to be able to verify depositors' claims, assess and collect each member institution's contribution, and make payouts to depositors. Paybox arrangements have no supervisory responsibilities or intervention powers. Nevertheless, they still require the ability to access information about members and need to have at their disposal sufficient funding and human resources to discharge their limited mandate.

A paybox system might operate under the auspices of the central bank, or the bank supervisory agency, or it could exist as an autonomous agency. Because a paybox is likely to become active only periodically, when bank failures trigger the need for depositor payouts, there are practical advantages to placing it under another agency. Thus, the number of permanent staff it will need to employ can be minimized, because personnel from the senior agency can be drafted to assist in the performance of its functions on an as-needed basis. It can also benefit from economies of scale in information technology and other support services by sharing with a larger agency.

A risk-minimizer deposit insurance agency has a broader mandate and needs correspondingly greater powers. These might include powers to control entry and exit in the deposit insurance system and to conduct examinations of members or to request that their affairs be examined by the primary supervisory authority. In

Table 1. Countries or Territories with Explicit, Limited Deposit Insurance Systems

Africa	Asia	Europe		Middle East	Western Hemisphere
Kenya	Bangladesh	Albania	Latvia	Algeria	Argentina
Nigeria	Hong Kong SAR	Austria	Lithuania	Bahrain	The Bahamas
Sudan	India	Belarus	Luxembourg	Jordan	Barbados
Tanzania	Indonesia	Belgium	Macedonia, FYR	Lebanon	Brazil
Uganda	Japan	Bulgaria	Malta	Morocco	Canada
Zimbabwe	Kazakhstan	Bosnia and Herzegovina	Netherlands	Oman	Chile
	Korea	Croatia	Norway		Colombia
	Marshall Islands	Cyprus	Poland		Dominican Republic
	Micronesia	Czech Republic	Portugal		Ecuador
	Philippines	Denmark	Romania		El Salvador
	Sri Lanka	Estonia	Russia		Guatemala
	Taiwan Province of China	Finland	Slovak Republic		Honduras
	Thailand	France	Slovenia		Jamaica
	Turkmenistan	Germany	Spain		Mexico
		Gibraltar	Sweden		Paraguay
		Greece	Switzerland		Peru
		Hungary	Turkey		Trinidad and Tobago
		Iceland	Ukraine		United States
		Ireland	United Kingdom		Venezuela
		Isle of Man			
		Italy			
6	14	40		6	19

Total: 85 countries/territories

Sources: Country authorities; and IMF staff.

some cases, deposit insurers may also have the power to set prudential regulations, have enforcement powers, and undertake regular or special examinations of their member institutions. However, the latter arrangement raises important issues about the coordination of supervisory authority and may lead to unnecessary duplication of supervisory effort, especially in countries where the supply of talented bank supervisors is limited. Deposit insurers may also potentially provide financial assistance, when required, to assist in the resolution of problem institutions. Unlike a central bank's lender of last resort role, however, a deposit insurance agency's support should be given only under strictly limited conditions (Box 2).

Between these two poles are a range of other possibilities. For example, a deposit insurance agency might have the power to intervene in banks, but lack the power to regulate them. It is also possible to envisage a gradual extension of the deposit insurance agency's powers over time. This happened in the United States, for example, where the Federal Deposit Insurance Corporation (FDIC) was initially established without direct supervisory authority of its own and gradually acquired it in cooperation with existing agencies.

The deposit insurer is best structured as an autonomous agency when its mandate is more extensive than that of a paybox. Whereas a paybox is dormant unless or until a depositor payout is triggered, a risk-minimizer needs to perform regular assessments of its member banks' financial condition. As a result, a risk-minimizer agency needs broader powers and a larger staff than a paybox. Moreover, where a deposit insurance agency has bank resolution powers of its own, it will need to ensure that it has staff with the relevant professional skills.

Responsibilities of Deposit Insurers

Mandates of deposit insurers may be considered "broad" (that is, they include some form of supervisory/regulatory tasks or involve the deposit insurance system in issues of financial assistance to problem institutions and bank resolution policies) or "narrow" (that is, the deposit insurance system is established as a paybox system, responsible only for collecting contributions from member banks and to pay out to depositors). Data were collected on these two categories (Table 2 and Statistical Appendix Table A2).

Table 2. Mandates and Powers of Deposit Insurance Agencies

	Total	Number of Observations	Share (In percent) 2004	2000
DIAs having broad responsibilities	46	84	55	49
DIAs making the decision to intervene in banks	18	83	22	...
DIAs with supervisory powers	16	81	20	...
Authority to determine premium rates				
DIA	40	77	52	...
Central bank	9	77	12	...
Separate supervisor	6	77	8	...
Other (ministry of finance/by law)	7	77	9	...
No information	8	77	10	...
Authority to act as liquidator and/or receiver	28	66	42	...
Active participation in failure resolution	33	69	48	...
Legal power to revoke insurance				
Fully on its own account	30	81	37	...
After approval/intervention by other agency	5	81	6	...
Right to take legal action against bank officials	40	84	48	...

Sources: Country sources; and IMF staff estimates.
Note: DIA = deposit insurance agency.

Roughly one-fifth of deposit insurance agencies are equipped with some form of supervisory authority, whereas approximately 50 percent have the authority to determine either the base premium rate or the risk-adjusted rate applied to individual banks. Most agencies having supervisory powers are either located in or closely connected to the banking supervisor. Consequently, arrangements such as that in the United States, where the FDIC exists as an autonomous agency with a full range of supervisory and intervention powers, are found only in a very few countries.

Mandates and powers, like other aspects of deposit insurance design, have evolved over time. Countries have tended to give broader responsibilities to deposit insurance agencies. In the majority of these cases, the agencies' mandates have been extended to the area of failure resolution and liquidation, possibly reflecting the growing recognition of the importance of early intervention and prompt corrective action for failing banks. Because the deposit insurance system's objective is to minimize net losses to the deposit insurance fund, particularly if it is given an explicit "least cost" mandate, assigning bank resolution powers to the deposit insurance agency may result in earlier intervention than otherwise would occur.

Interagency Coordination

The nature and the extent of the coordination needed between the different agencies responsible for operating the financial safety net will vary according to a country's specific institutional arrangements.

When a single agent (generally the central bank) acts simultaneously as lender of last resort, banking supervisor, and deposit insurer, coordination is an internal matter within a single organization. When, however, the functions of lender of last resort, banking supervisor, and deposit insurer are allocated to separate agencies, coordination may be more complex, because each agency will be held accountable for discharging its own mandate. As a consequence, various issues related to information sharing, allocation of powers and responsibilities, and coordination among the different functions need to be clearly and explicitly addressed in order to promote and maintain the credibility of the safety net. The relevant laws and statutes need to specify quite clearly the respective agencies' ability to request and share information, and sufficient legal "gateways" need to be created to ensure, for example, that the deposit insurance agency has access to bank supervisory data on a timely basis. The implementation of the information-sharing arrangements provided for by law might be underpinned by the agreement of a memorandum of understanding among the relevant agencies.

Membership

Sound Practice: Membership criteria should seek to avoid adverse selection and limit risk taking.

All institutions that are admitted into the deposit insurance system should be explicitly authorized to

Table 3. Number and Share of Compulsory Regimes
(In percent of all deposit insurance systems)

Region	1995		2000		2004	
	Total	In percent	Total	In percent	Total	In percent
Africa	4	100	4	80	5	83
Asia	4	57	7	70	10	71
Europe	11	48	31	97	39	95
Middle East	1	50	4	100	6	100
Americas	6	55	16	94	18	95
Total	**26**	**55**	**62**	**91**	**78**	**91**

Source: Statistical Appendix Table A3.

take deposits and be subject to the same levels of stringent regulatory oversight. This condition helps control the system's potential risk exposure and hence ensures its financial viability.

An additional measure to strengthen the financial viability of the deposit insurance system is to make membership compulsory for all eligible institutions. Compulsory membership avoids the possibility that only the weakest institutions join the deposit insurance system, jeopardizing the financial viability of the system. Compulsory membership does involve some degree of cross-subsidization by financially strong institutions of weak ones, but subsidy is inherent in all forms of insurance. With compulsory membership, all members benefit from having a more stable financial system with reduced fears of depositor runs.

Among the reasons voluntary systems fail is that either their funding base is insufficiently diversified, or only comparatively more risky institutions tend to join, with stronger institutions opting not to become members. This tends to mean that over time voluntary systems are not financially viable and are often undermined by adverse selection. Hence, compulsory membership is preferred.

The survey of deposit insurance practice shows that by the year 2000, compulsory membership existed in 91 percent of deposit insurance systems (Table 3). The only major change to have occurred was in the Dominican Republic, which in 2002 replaced a very limited protection system with a compulsory contingency fund (Fondo de Contingencia). Although the fund is primarily for recapitalizing banks, it also functions like a deposit insurance scheme in that it can initiate operations once a bank fails.

Membership is mandatory in all countries that have introduced deposit insurance systems since 2000, except for Sudan and Russia. However, Russia has issued regulations stating that, at the end of a planned transition period, banks not admitted to the system will lose their right to take retail deposits.[10]

State-Owned Banks

State-owned banks that take deposits should be required to participate in the deposit insurance system. Although it might be argued that limited deposit insurance may not be credible in the case of these institutions because they already enjoy an implicit government guarantee of their deposits, including these institutions within the deposit insurance system helps broaden the deposit insurance system's funding base. It also removes one potential source of competitive distortion between these institutions and private banks, although many other forms of competitive distortion will, of course, continue to exist.

Foreign Banks

In principle, branches of foreign banks or their locally incorporated subsidiaries should be included in the deposit insurance system. Although foreign banks may have the backing of the home country parent, this reputation factor alone is usually sufficient to ensure

---

[10]In general, Russia provides a good counterexample for the typical characteristics of recently introduced deposit insurance systems. First, whereas most countries decide to make insurance eligible for households and for (at least) small and medium-sized companies, Russia's scheme protects only household deposits. Second, an extensive screening process for each bank wanting to participate was set in place. In 2004, after the banking sector had experienced renewed problems, a law was passed that provides for central bank compensation of household deposits in banks not admitted to the scheme. Finally, the Russian deposit insurance system was subject to several exclusions, in particular for the state-owned Sberbank, whose deposits will continue to be covered by a full state guarantee for several years.

Box 1. Sound Deposit Insurance Practices

Explicit deposit insurance has a number of important advantages compared with implicit insurance.

The authorities need with be clear about their objectives in establishing a deposit insurance system.

Coverage levels should be set at levels that are consistent with the deposit insurance system's objectives and that can be supported by available funding.

The commitment to depositor protection should be backed by adequate funding.

Membership criteria should ensure that the deposit insurance system can remain financially viable on an ongoing basis.

When combined with other factors, like effective regulation and supervision, specific design features of the deposit insurance system can significantly reduce the risk of moral hazard.

A deposit insurance agency's legal powers and human and financial resources need to be appropriate to its mandate, and its actions should be well co-coordinated with those of other safety net players.

The efficiency and effectiveness of deposit insurance systems are enhanced by

- laying down their functions and powers by statute or contract;
- stating explicitly the membership criteria and the degree of protection that the scheme does, and does not, offer; and
- taking measures to promote public awareness of the existence of depositor protection.

The advantages of an explicit, limited deposit insurance system can best be realized if certain essential preconditions are in place.

---

that many leading international banks will stand behind their locally incorporated subsidiaries.

There are good reasons for requiring foreign-owned subsidiaries and branches of foreign banks to become members of the deposit insurance system:

- Inclusion of foreign branches increases the funding base and avoids competitive inequality.
- Comfort letters, often required by authorities stating that the parent stands behind the subsidiary, do not create an enforceable legal obligation to support the subsidiary.
- Experience suggests that foreign parent banks may be reluctant to support their subsidiaries if the financial crisis in the local market is especially severe.
- The parent bank itself may fail (as have Barings, Bank of Credit and Commerce International, and other large international banks). If this happens, it is unlikely that the home country deposit insurance system would extend to depositors with the bank's local operations.[11]
- Some jurisdictions, such as the United States, require that the worldwide assets of a failed bank be frozen and used to cover home deposits first.

Nonbank Deposit-Taking Institutions

An inherent tension exists between the desire to establish a broad-based system, in which the deposit insurers' risks are diversified among a large number of institutions, and the importance of ensuring that all institutions are subject to adequate supervision. In those countries

where only institutions that are authorized as banks can take deposits, only authorized banks will be eligible to become members of the system. However, in some countries, institutions other than banks—for example, credit unions or savings and loan institutions—may be permitted to take deposits. If these institutions are unregulated, they could expose the deposit insurance system to heightened risks of failure. In this case, an alternative is to establish a separate system for different categories of institutions. Particularly when the deposit insurance system is structured as a mutual guarantee system, the membership should be sufficiently restricted that it is possible for member institutions to engage in a degree of mutual surveillance.

Coverage

Sound Practice: Coverage should be set at levels that are consistent with the deposit insurance system's objectives and that can be supported by available funding.

Setting appropriate and credible limits to coverage is a central design feature of an explicit deposit insurance system.[12] Deposit insurance system credibility will be strengthened if the level of coverage is seen by the public as consistent with its objectives and with the source and level of available funding. Moreover, as discussed below, the coverage level is an important factor in determining whether market discipline is undermined or not. There are two aspects to the subject of deposit coverage: monetary limits and scope of coverage.

---

[11]Special arrangements exist among the member countries of the European Union. Under the principle of home country control, depositors with the branch of a bank incorporated in another member state will be covered by the home state's deposit insurance scheme. Banks can, however, opt to become members of the host state scheme if this provides more generous coverage levels.

[12]Statistical Appendix Table A6 gives an overview of the actual coverage levels, in domestic currency, in U.S. dollars, and relative to per capita GDP.

Box 2. Deposit Insurance Agencies and the Financial Support of Troubled Banks

When the failure of a bank could cause widespread adverse effects on economic conditions or financial stability, the government or central bank would be expected to address the issue. If the deposit insurer is to support troubled banks in such a situation, it should do so only on the request and with the guarantee of the government. Moreover, providing financial assistance to a troubled bank may exacerbate the deposit insurer's financial condition. To avoid inappropriate financial support to troubled banks, the deposit insurer should require that the following three conditions are met.

- *Least cost.* The deposit insurer must establish that financial assistance is the least costly to the insurance fund of all possible methods for resolving the institution (for example, liquidated payout, purchase, and assumption transaction). In most cases, bank closing proposals are less costly to the insurance fund. Requiring the least costly method in resolving a failing institution will provide greater incentives for an insured bank's shareholders and large creditors to impose more discipline on management to operate safely and soundly.

- *Management competence.* The deposit insurer should either require new management or ensure that the existing management is competent; has complied with all applicable laws, rules, and supervisory directives and orders; and has never engaged in any insider dealings, speculative practices, or other abusive activity.

- *No benefit to former shareholders.* The deposit insurer must ensure that the ownership interest is diluted to a nominal amount. Ideally, any support should be matched by a private sector capital infusion. The deposit insurer must ensure that shareholders of failing institutions do not benefit from the assistance provided by the government.

Monetary Limits

Most systems set limits on the size of deposits that qualify for protection.[13] In general, a deposit insurance system that focuses on the objective of protecting small-scale depositors provides a relatively low level of coverage, designed primarily to compensate unsophisticated depositors with transaction balances and modest savings. By contrast, a deposit insurance system that emphasizes the objective of preserving financial system stability may cover a larger portion of deposits. In the latter case, how-

ever, care should be taken not to offer such high coverage levels that depositors who otherwise would have both the incentive and the ability to influence risk taking by bank management (for example, institutional investors) would be discouraged from doing so.

When examining coverage levels, some studies have used the average coverage level of one to two times per capita GDP, cited in several surveys by the IMF, as a guide to optimal coverage levels. That ratio, however, is only a statistical description of deposit insurance systems and is not meant to be considered as a desired design feature. Good reasons may exist for setting a particular coverage level either above or below the world average. Figure 1 plots coverage ratios against per capita GDP in 2003 for all countries with coverage ratios below 10 times per capita GDP. The correlation coefficient between per capita GDP and coverage levels indicates that countries tend to cluster into three groups:

(1) a small cluster with very high coverage levels and low per capita income;

(2) a large group of developed countries with coverage ratios ranging from zero to three times; and

(3) a very large number of low- and medium-income countries clustering near the origin.

The correlation coefficient between per capita GDP and the coverage ratio is −0.29 for the whole sample, and −0.28 for the sample excluding those countries with ratios above five times per capita GDP. This result tends to confirm the widely held perception that there is an inverse relationship between a country's per capita income and the relative generosity of the coverage limits in its deposit insurance system.

Before setting the coverage level, several policy and structural features should be considered, including

- determining that the coverage is consistent with the objectives of the deposit insurance system and with the funds available;

- setting coverage levels that take into account the incentives for wealthy and sophisticated investors to participate in monitoring activities and exert market discipline; and

- preventing possibilities of excessive coverage, such as establishing limits on "double coverage" arising from holding several accounts in the same bank, all below the coverage limit (this problem can be mitigated by specifying that coverage is "per depositor" not "per deposit").

Coverage limits could be set to cover a given percentage of deposits by number and by value. To make this determination, the authorities will need information on the size distribution of deposits in the system. For example, if deposits are distributed between a large number of relatively small deposits and a small number of very large deposits, it might be feasible to aim to cover approximately 80 percent of the number of deposits, but only approximately 20 percent by value.

---

[13]The main exception is Germany's deposit insurance system, which combines a public, limited deposit insurance scheme with a system of mutual guarantees among the banks. The newly introduced public and compulsory regime provides coverage up to €20,000, the level specified in the 1994 EU directive. Any amount above that threshold is covered by the private scheme offered by banks. The latter provides coverage that in principle is unlimited.

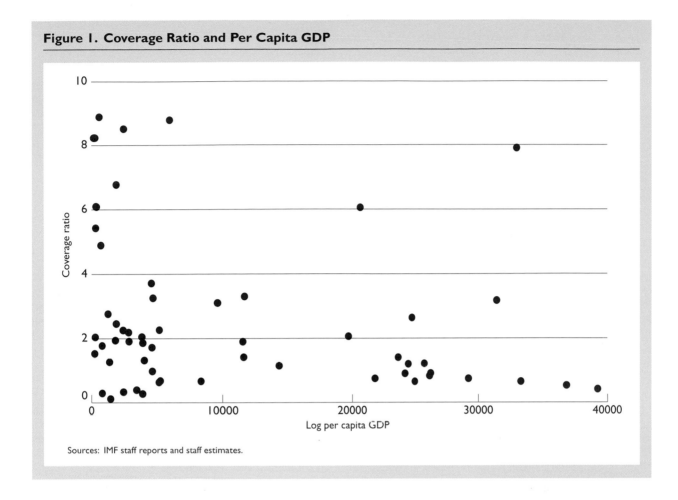

Figure 1. Coverage Ratio and Per Capita GDP

Sources: IMF staff reports and staff estimates.

A number of countries have successfully followed this practice (see Statistical Appendix Table A6). The objectives of the deposit insurance system are also a relevant factor to consider. If the deposit insurance system has the objective of protecting small-scale depositors, it might aim to cover a relatively large percentage of deposits by number, but a much smaller percentage by value; one with a financial stability objective might aim to cover a higher percentage both by number and, especially, by value.

A further factor in deciding on the coverage level is to take into account the deposit insurance system's available funding. Scenarios can be constructed to assess the resource implications of the failure of a sample of banks given the proposed coverage level. If these scenarios suggest that adequate funding for the deposit guarantee will not be available, the proposed coverage level will probably need to be adjusted downward. Offering high levels of coverage without considering the means by which the deposit guarantee is to be honored undermines the credibility of the system. Moreover, excessively high coverage levels increase the probability that the banking system alone will be unable to fund the deposit guarantee.

Coverage may also need to be increased from time to time to take into account the impact of inflation. In this context, some countries index the coverage level to inflation or are considering such a step (for example, the Dominican Republic, El Salvador, Peru, and Romania). Although countries with very high inflation may have few other options, indexing reduces transparency to the public. Indexing coverage levels makes it difficult for the public to keep abreast of frequent changes in the level. A viable alternative is, therefore, to specify a procedure as to when and how coverage limits should be reviewed, but few countries currently have such a system in place.

Current Trends in Coverage Levels

Between 1998 and 2004, the average coverage ratio increased, from 2.4 times per capita GDP in 1998 to 2.7 (Table 4). The upward drift in coverage ratios reflects both adjustments within existing systems and the introduction of new systems with relatively high coverage.

Countries with unusually high coverage levels (above five times GDP per capita) typically experienced recent financial fragility (Table 4). Among these countries, one group has rolled back a blanket guarantee (for example,

Table 4. Summary Statistics for Coverage Ratios

Region	Average 1998	Average 2004	Standard Deviation 1998	Standard Deviation 2004	Share above 3 1998	Share above 3 2004	Share below 1 1998	Share below 1 2004
Africa	4.31	2.14	2.72	2.08	0.50	0.33	0.00	0.50
Asia[1]	4.67	2.02	2.02	1.17	0.71	0.00	0.00	0.00
Europe	1.56	2.19	1.68	2.19	0.10	0.24	0.47	0.37
Middle East	3.40	3.07	...	3.17	...	0.50	...	0.50
Americas[2]	3.20	6.18	2.25	14.34	0.42	0.53	0.08	0.06
Total	**2.45**	**2.67**	**2.34**	**2.50**	**0.17**	**0.32**	**0.32**	**0.29**

Source: Statistical Appendix Table A6.
[1]Excluding the Marshall Islands and Micronesia.
[2]Excluding Ecuador and Mexico.

Mexico), or using the deposit insurance system as a de facto substitute for a full guarantee (in particular, Paraguay, which has a coverage ratio of 9.3 percent; Turkey, 9.4 percent; Honduras, 9.7 percent; Macedonia, FYR, 10 percent; and Nicaragua, 41 percent). For countries like Japan, the coverage ratio of 2.6 percent of per capita GDP is understated, because the deposit insurance refers only to time deposits, whereas deposits for payment and settlement still enjoy full coverage. Finally, coverage levels are very high in the Marshall Islands and Micronesia (because deposits there are covered by the U.S. FDIC). Many of the countries with recent increases in coverage levels are in Central and Eastern Europe, and modified their deposit insurance systems to comply with the requirements of EU membership.[14] Because the coverage levels set in the European Union's directive on deposit insurance were set initially for countries with relatively more developed financial systems, their application in the new EU entrants and candidate countries gives rise to coverage that is high relative to per capita GDP, although economic growth may erode this anomaly over time. A second group that has raised coverage levels significantly consists of four Latin American countries (the Dominican Republic, Colombia, El Salvador, and Peru). Here, it appears that the desire to stabilize depositor confidence in a fragile environment has played a central role, and thus deposit insurance is a partial substitute for a full blanket guarantee.

A few countries have lowered their coverage ratios since 1998. Two groups can be distinguished in this category. On the one hand, some developed countries have reduced their coverage from very high levels—for example, Norway, after having completed the stabilization of its banking system. On the other

hand, several developing countries have experienced erosion in coverage, mainly owing to a combination of relatively high inflation and the slow adjustment of coverage limits.

Scope of Coverage

Deposit insurance systems have different levels of scope and coverage. Issues include the type of depositors covered, the currency denomination of protected deposits, coverage of government deposits and coverage of deposits of "insiders."

Depositor Coverage

The authorities must decide if a system's coverage applies only to deposits placed by households or natural persons, or whether deposits placed by incorporated entities should also be included. The decision depends, in part, on the objective of the deposit insurance system. Those systems designed to protect small-scale depositors may exclude incorporated entities, whereas those seeking to support financial sector stability may include them. In this latter case, the capital and working balances of small businesses gain some protection. This is often thought to be a desirable policy goal in itself, all the more so when many small businesses may be less financially sophisticated than some individual depositors. Extending coverage to small businesses may encourage them to use the banking system rather than transacting business exclusively in cash.

On the other hand, if all corporations benefit from deposit protection, market discipline may suffer. If explicit deposit insurance does reduce market discipline to the extent implied by recent econometric studies, excluding incorporated entities might well be considered a partial policy response. An alternative approach would be to exclude only medium and large

---

[14]Many countries amended their law, stating the exact increase in well-specified periods. By 2007, most countries will have reached the minimum of €20,000 required by the 1994 EU directive.

Table 5. Number and Share of Deposit Insurance Systems Exclusively Covering Households and Small and Medium-Sized Enterprises

Region	1995 Total	1995 In percent	2000 Total	2000 In percent	2004 Total	2004 In percent
Africa	1	25	0	0	1	17
Asia	0	0	2	20	2	17
Europe	5	22	12	38	17	40
Middle East	0	0	0	0	0	0
Americas	0	0	4	24	2	10
Total	**6**	**13**	**18**	**26**	**22**	**26**

Source: Statistical Appendix Table A6.

corporations from coverage. Currently, at least eight countries in the sample follow that practice (Austria, Belgium, Estonia, Ireland, Luxembourg, the Netherlands, Poland, and the United Kingdom).

Recent trends point in two contrary directions. Several countries have extended the coverage of their system to new types of deposits or depositors (a detailed account is provided in Statistical Appendix Tables A1 and A6). In particular, several deposit insurance systems now include private companies and legal entities, instead of granting insurance exclusively to natural persons or households. However, since a number of new systems have chosen to restrict eligibility to natural persons, the share of systems excluding incorporated bodies has stayed constant since 2000. This is compared with the previous five years in which the number of systems being extended to legal persons had doubled (Table 5).

The decision to exclude interbank deposits is clearer than the decision to exclude the deposits of incorporated entities. An important source of market discipline arises from banks monitoring the behavior of other banks. Therefore, banks need to be exposed to the risk of loss for funds placed with each other. Relatively low coverage levels help to provide the incentives for mutual surveillance by banks, because most interbank deposits are of a size that only a relatively small proportion would be covered by a deposit insurance system with appropriately low limits. However, a further mechanism to reinforce market discipline is to explicitly exclude interbank deposits from system coverage. The survey results reveal that the share of deposit insurance systems explicitly excluding interbank claims has risen sharply, from 45 percent in 1995 to 79 percent in 2000 and to 86 percent in 2004 (Table 6). In addi-

Table 6. Share of Deposit Insurance Systems Excluding Interbank and Foreign Currency Deposits
(In percent)

Region	1995 Interbank	1995 Foreign currency	2000 Interbank	2000 Foreign currency	2004 Interbank	2004 Foreign currency
Africa	75	75	40	60	67	50
Asia	71	43	70	50	79	57
Europe	48	17	97	38	98	10
Middle East	0	0	50	25	83	50
Americas	18	9	71	29	74	21
Total	**45**	**23**	**79**	**38**	**86**	**24**

Source: Statistical Appendix Table A7.

tion, some countries generally including incorporated entities disqualify other types of financial intermediaries; for example, insurance or asset management companies. Such a policy can be expected to further strengthen monitoring efforts by the private sector, complementing such measures as the exclusion of large corporations. Although the tendency to exclude interbank liabilities is welcomed in principle, its effect will probably be moderate in countries with relatively low coverage levels.

Foreign Currency Deposits

Recent econometric work has treated both foreign currency and interbank coverage symmetrically,[15] but the arguments for and against inclusion may differ, both in content and in complexity. Although interbank liabilities are usually excluded from coverage in deposit insurance systems, the decision to exclude foreign currency deposits will strongly depend on country circumstances. Where most transactions are conducted in the domestic currency and the total value of retail foreign currency deposits is small, the authorities may choose not to cover foreign currency deposits without risking financial instability. However, in countries where foreign currency deposits make up a significant share of retail deposits, the inclusion of such deposits in the deposit insurance system is a prerequisite for reducing the risk of small-scale depositors triggering bank runs. Moreover, the deposit insurance system is unlikely to achieve its financial stability objective if foreign currency deposits form a significant proportion of the deposit base but are excluded from the system. Where foreign currency deposits are widely used for transactions and savings purposes, the authorities may have little choice but to include them within the deposit insurance coverage on depositor protection grounds.

Guaranteeing that deposits will be repaid in foreign-currency exposes the deposit insurer to risks that are not easily managed. At a minimum, the deposit insurance agency must have access to an adequate level of foreign-currency-denominated assets to make good on the guarantee and must be able to monitor and measure its foreign exchange risks. An alternative approach is to pass the foreign exchange risk from the deposit insurer to the depositor. In this case, foreign currency deposits would be covered but the depositor would be repaid in domestic currency. In this event, the law or regulation governing coverage must specify the conversion from foreign to domestic currency will be made at the exchange rate that prevails at some uniform and clearly specified time.

A development common to new and existing systems is an increasing tendency to make foreign currency

---

[15]For example, see Cull, Senbet, and Sorge (2006) on the construction of moral hazard indices.

Table 7. Share of Deposit Insurance Systems Explicitly Excluding Government, Insider, and Criminal Deposits

	2000		2004	
	Total	In percent	Total	In percent
Government	33	46	57	66
Insiders	34	47	54	63
Criminal	23	32	55	64

Source: Statistical Appendix Table A7.

---

deposits eligible, while explicitly excluding interbank liabilities. Almost 90 percent of systems now exclude interbank deposits, whereas approximately 75 percent cover foreign currency deposits. In systems established since 2000, two-thirds cover deposits in foreign currency, whereas only one system (Bosnia and Herzegovina) includes interbank claims.

Other Exclusions

Government deposits and deposits placed by "insiders" (that is, bank owners or managers or closely connected persons) are typically excluded from coverage. Government deposits are likely to significantly exceed coverage limits in most systems, but in any case government departments and government agencies should have an incentive to monitor the condition of the banks with which public deposits are placed. Moreover, excluding these deposits prevents the limited resources of the deposit insurance fund—which will have been accumulated by premiums charged on the banking sector—from being used to provide a de facto subsidy to the public sector. The exclusion of insider deposits serves some important purposes:

- It provides owners and managers with an additional incentive to avoid excessive risk taking by exposing their deposits with the bank to the risk of loss.
- It reduces both the potential for conflicts of interest and the scope for asset stripping that could occur if insiders were able to grant themselves loans that would be held at the bank in the form of insured deposits.

Table 7 shows a strong trend to state explicitly in law that these claims are not eligible; nearly all of the recently introduced systems include such clauses. Similar arguments can be used to justify the exclusion of deposits held by those responsible for auditing the bank or deposits placed by directors of other companies in the same group.[16] In addition, many countries have amended their laws particularly to exclude from coverage deposits relating to criminal activity. This trend may reflect, in part, recent efforts to combat money laundering.

Funding

Sound Practice: The commitment to depositor protection should be backed by adequate funding.

The funding arrangements for the deposit insurance system should assure depositors that the guarantee will be honored and that they will be able to obtain prompt access to their funds. This requires that the nature and sources of the system's funding be clearly understood by both the authorities and the general public, and the funds to back the deposit guarantee be readily available. In addition, the deposit insurance system should be sufficiently well funded that depositors are able to obtain compensation promptly; otherwise, one of the key benefits of deposit insurance compared with the operation of insolvency law will not be realized.

There are three aspects of funding for a deposit insurance system:
- reserve fund—including ex post, ex ante, and initial funding;
- premium and funding base; and
- supplemental or emergency funding.

Reserve Fund

Deposit insurance system can be funded using either ex post or ex ante systems.

Ex Post Funding

An ex post funding system establishes the deposit insurance system as a loss-sharing or mutual guarantee arrangement among the participating institutions. This arrangement does not rely on a fund accumulated ex ante, but instead relies on guarantees offered by participating institutions to cover depositors once the bank has failed.[17] Although mutual guarantee systems are generally privately organized and administered, there are also examples of publicly operated ex post systems that have the characteristics of a mutual guarantee arrangement.

In the event of the failure of an individual institution, the other participating institutions are assessed ex post for contributions to the deposit insurance system. One advantage of such a system is that it should induce the banks to monitor each other's activities and thereby offset the weakening of market discipline that might otherwise occur through the creation of a deposit insurance system. Another advantage, in environments where the quality of transparency and enforcement practices is low, is that it reduces the opportunities for misappropriation by government authorities of funds accumulated by the deposit insurance system.

A disadvantage of this arrangement is that the funds are not collected beforehand, introducing delays and making this arrangement less dependable. In addition, ex post funding might prove to be time inconsistent. Because bank failures normally occur in situations of weak macroeconomic fundamentals, honoring commitments to a deposit insurance system may exacerbate the banks' financial condition and lead to a domino effect of bank failures. This could lead to possible renegotiations of the terms and conditions of funding the deposit insurance system, or perhaps even the collapse of the deposit insurance system. In other words, ex post funding might prove to have procyclical effects, since levies will have to be raised in situations where balance sheets have already deteriorated. It thus has the potential to contribute further to financial fragility.

Ex Ante Funding

The alternative model is to accumulate an ex ante reserve fund for the purpose of compensating depositors through the regular payment of premiums by institutions with insured liabilities. In this case, the administration of the deposit insurance system is typically in the hands of a public agency created for the purpose, although the fund administrator might also be a private agency.

An ex ante fund has a number of advantages. First, public confidence may be enhanced by the existence of a fund. In particular, it allows for a prompt reimbursement of depositors, preventing the possibility of a loss of confidence owing to delayed compensation payments. Second, ex ante systems have the ability to smooth premium payments over the economic cycle, reducing the risk that banks will face demands for contributions at a time when their balance sheets are already under stress. In addition, ex ante funding could incorporate risk-adjusted premiums by the deposit insurance agency, providing one of several mechanisms that can be used to reduce moral hazard (see Section III).

One of the main disadvantages of an ex ante fund is that in a highly concentrated banking system it may be difficult to establish a fund of sufficient size that the deposit guarantee would be credible.

The survey results show that between 1995 and 2004, the number of ex ante funded systems rose sharply, from

---

[16]See, for example, the exclusions specified in Annex 1(7) of the EU deposit insurance directive.

[17]The first deposit insurance scheme to be established, created by the state of New York in 1829, was explicitly modeled on the practice that required Cantonese merchants who held special charters to trade with foreigners to be liable for one another's debts.

Table 8. Number and Share of Prefunded Systems
(In percent of all deposit insurance systems)

Region	1995		2000		2004	
	Total	In percent	Total	In percent	Total	In percent
Africa	4	100	4	80	6	100
Asia	7	100	10	100	11	79
Europe	13	57	25	78	32	78
Middle East	1	50	3	75	5	83
Americas	9	82	16	94	18	95
Total	**34**	**72**	**58**	**85**	**72**	**84**

Source: Statistical Appendix Table A4.

34 to 72 (Table 8). The tendency to raise premiums ex ante is particularly common for deposit insurance systems that have been recently introduced. Among the new systems established since 2000, only three small countries (Liechtenstein, Isle of Man, and Slovenia), two of them mini-states with a relatively small fraction of deposits held by residents, rely primarily on ex post funding. In addition, a few systems that had formerly relied on ex post funding have partly changed their approach in recent years (for example, Germany in 1998 and France in 1999).

The fact that ex ante funding is preferred by many countries stands in sharp contrast to some recent academic literature that has argued that this practice aggravates the problem of increased risk taking by banks in the presence of an explicit deposit insurance system (see, for example, Demirgüç-Kunt and Kane, 2002). It is argued in this literature that prefunding the deposit insurance system will lead to increased risk taking, because funds are already "earmarked" for insolvency resolution, thus giving depositors a false sense of safety. In addition, opponents of prefunding point out that funds already contributed to a system might be considered as sunk costs, decreasing the propensity of banks to participate in private monitoring arrangements. Finally, concerns have also been expressed that in weak institutional environments, the creation of a deposit insurance fund will simply provide an opportunity for looting by corrupt officials.

Considerations in Establishing an Ex Ante Fund

If an ex ante fund is created, an important issue concerns the target size of the fund and the contribution rates that will be required from the banks. One possible method for deciding on the target size of the fund is to estimate its average expected losses based on historical loss experience over a recent three- to four-year period.[18] This method could be adopted with varying degrees of sophistication, ranging from a rough estimation based on recent bank failures to simulations using advanced statistical techniques. However, it will be difficult to apply this method where the banking system has gone through rapid transformation (for example, post-crisis restructuring), or a limited-size banking system, with the result that historical loss experience will be a minimal guide to the future.

An alternative approach is to use survey evidence, which indicates that most countries with an ex ante funded deposit insurance system have established funds in the range of 3 percent of total deposits, with some setting a fund size of 1.25 percent of deposits and others as much as 5 percent of deposits. This provides a range of possible targets for the size of the fund, but—as with the coverage issue—this range of possibilities should not be treated as an inflexible rule.

In determining a target size for the fund, the authorities will also need to take into account the capacity of the banking system to contribute to the creation and maintenance of a fund. If the fund target size is set too high, then the contribution rates needed to build a fund in a reasonable period of time may be more than the banking system is able to absorb. The additional burden represented by the deposit insurance contributions could jeopardize bank profitability, particularly when banking sector profitability is already weak. In any case, the level of contributions required of the banks should always be set with a view to their impact on banks' profitability and hence retained earnings, bearing in mind the principle that a profitable banking sector is generally a sound one.

---

[18]Average loss experience over this length of time provides a better indication of expected losses than those experienced in any one year, because bank failures tend to occur in clusters and are often linked to the economic cycle.

The authorities will also need to decide the time-scale over which the ex ante fund will be accumulated. Attempting to accumulate a fund too rapidly will place the same contribution burden on the banks as would targeting too large a fund. On the other hand, the authorities may wish to see a fund in place relatively soon after the announcement of the creation of a deposit insurance system to encourage the public perception of a credible deposit guarantee. One way in which these objectives can be reconciled is for the fund to be started with a capital contribution by the government (for example, in the form of government bonds), which can then be retired as the banking sector begins to make its own contribution to the system. However, there must be a realistic timetable for retiring the public funds; otherwise, the government support will become a quasi-permanent feature of the deposit insurance system. This will defeat one of the objectives of establishing a deposit insurance system, which is to ensure that a large part of the cost of dealing with bank failures falls on the banking system itself.

A further issue for an ex ante deposit insurance system concerns the investment policy for the resources of the fund. The maximization of investment returns should not be an objective in the management of the fund. Rather, the fund resources must be invested in instruments that are

- secure;
- highly liquid; and
- not subject to possible unavailability in the event of a financial crisis.

For these reasons investments in government bonds and bills, together with remunerated deposits with the central bank, are frequently used as investment instruments for a deposit insurance fund. Placing funds with domestic banks exposes the deposit insurance system to the risk that its funds may not be available when most needed or creates the risk that the deposit insurer could itself trigger a liquidity crisis at some banks when it withdraws its deposits with them to meet the claims of depositors with a failed bank. In some circumstances—for example, where the deposit insurance system needs access to foreign-currency-denominated assets—it may be prudent to invest at least some of its resources in the bonds of foreign governments. Following the same investment rule as for central bank reserves provides one way of ensuring that fund assets are invested wisely. The investment policies of the fund and an audited balance sheet should be published from time to time and otherwise made publicly available.

Premiums and Funding Base

Three factors determine the funding base of the deposit insurance system: (1) the premium levels; (2) the deposit base for assessing premiums; and (3)

supplementary financing provided by the government. These factors must be considered together and designed to ensure that the deposit insurance system funding is credible and stable.

Types of Premiums—Flat-Rate versus Risk-Based

The two most common methods for assessing members of the deposit insurance system are flat-rate and risk-based premiums. The primary advantage of a flat-rate premium is that assessments can easily be calculated and administered. An argument in favor of a risk-based system is that it explicitly prices the risks taken by the banks. Depository institutions can increase the risk to their portfolios but incur additional insurance expenses.

The primary advantage of a flat-rate premium is ease of administration. Administration includes assessment of risks, collection, and audit of premiums. Because designing and monitoring a risk-based system is technically difficult and requires skilled and experienced staff, many newly established or transitional deposit insurance systems initially adopt flat-rate deposit insurance assessments.

Once the financial sector and deposit insurance system has matured, the deposit insurance system may consider implementing risk-based premiums. Risk-based premiums, by definition, are based on the risk a particular financial institution poses to the deposit insurance system. There are several different methods to attempt to quantify this risk, including capital ratios, supervisory subgroups (based primarily on the CAMELS bank supervision methodology), level of nonperforming loans, or combinations.

Theoretically, well-designed risk-based premiums will be more actuarially fair. In a flat-rate system, low-risk banks effectively subsidize the benefits for high-risk institutions, and loss burdens are spread disproportionately among insured banks. Risk-based premiums should eventually diminish the strong bank subsidization of weaker banks, as well as the moral hazard problems.

Risk-Adjusted Insurance Premiums

Like coinsurance, the idea of risk-adjusted premiums is borrowed from the provision of commercial insurance: the greater the insurance risk, the greater the insurance premium. In a risk-related system of insurance premiums, banks pay a fee based on their relative risk of failure; banks that engage in riskier behavior would be subject to higher premiums. If the risk of failure is priced properly, the benefits of increased risk taking will be taxed away, limiting banks' incentive to engage in overly risky activities. This should in turn lead banks to limit their risk exposure and therefore act as a correction to the erosion of market discipline resulting from the introduction of deposit insurance.

Table 9. Number and Share of Deposit Insurance Systems Using Risk-Adjusted Premiums

Region	1995		2000		2004	
	Total	In percent	Total	In percent	Total	In percent
Africa	0	0	0	0	0	0
Asia	2	29	4	40	3	21
Europe	0	0	12	38	13	32
Middle East	0	0	0	0	1	17
Americas	2	18	8	47	7	37
Total	**4**	**9**	**24**	**35**	**24**	**28**

Source: Statistical Appendix Table A5.

Risk-adjusted deposit insurance premiums restore an element of market discipline because riskier institutions are required to pay higher premiums than conservative ones. The second half of the 1990s saw a strong increase in the proportion of deposit insurance systems using risk-adjusted premiums, from 9 percent in 1995 to 35 percent in 2000 (Table 9).

There is, however, wide variation in the practice of risk adjustment. Most countries that have risk-adjusted premiums use a variant of the CAMELS system to sort banks into different risk groups, often with an emphasis on capital adequacy (for example, Canada, Colombia, France, and Hong Kong SAR). Countries such as Finland, Hungary, Portugal, and Sweden rely exclusively on solvency or capital adequacy ratios. In some regimes, the risk premium is a largely discretionary choice by the banking supervisor or the central bank (for example, in Nicaragua and Romania). A few countries (for example, Colombia) apply risk-adjustment premiums by giving sound banks a refund on a portion of their premiums. Some countries regularly assess risks, whereas others apply higher rates only under special conditions, often determined by the banking supervisor. For example, the deposit insurance system in El Salvador applies a markup of 50 percent if the bank has substandard securities or is subject to intervention or special supervision.

Moreover, since 2000 the trend toward using risk-adjusted premiums has been partially reversed. Although some already existing deposit insurance systems (for example, in Colombia and Taiwan Province of China) have introduced risk adjustment, others (for example, in Kazakhstan; Macedonia, FYR; Mexico; and Romania) have opted to use a flat rate, even though the respective laws and regulations give them the option to adjust premium rates according to risk. In addition, only a very few countries that have established deposit insurance systems since 2000 have decided to apply risk-adjusted premiums (for example, Algeria, Hong Kong SAR, and Nicaragua). A consequence of these trends is that the share of deposit insurance systems using risk-adjusted premiums has fallen from 35 percent to 28 percent since 2000 (see Table 9).

The reversal in the trends toward risk-adjusted premiums reflects the practical difficulties involved in implementing them. First, a policy of premium differentiation requires a number of preconditions probably not present in many of the countries that have recently adopted a deposit insurance system. In particular, accurate supervisory information must be obtained in a timely manner and processed using quite sophisticated risk assessment techniques. Second, the required risk assessment technologies might not be available or applicable given a lack of monitoring resources. In such a situation, it will be difficult to properly differentiate among different risk classes. Finally, in order to set meaningful risk-based insurance premiums, the deposit insurer must not only be able to assess the current value of a bank's assets and liabilities (already a difficult matter where no market exists for them), but must be able to assess how much a bank's net worth will change under a variety of different scenarios.

These considerations suggest that although risk-adjusted premiums may be attractive in principle, they are administratively demanding and are unlikely to work well unless supported by complementary policies, for example prompt bank intervention and effective supervision and regulation. Nonetheless, the average level of the required premium needs to be commensurate with the level of risk, in order to ensure the financial viability of the deposit insurance system and to enhance its credibility.

Deposit Base

Most deposit insurance systems use deposits as the base on which to charge premiums or calculate the levy needed to compensate depositors under ex post assessments. It is administratively simpler for the fund to charge premiums on all of the deposits, and 23 countries in the sample (or 33 percent) do so. Some authorities, however, consider it inequitable to charge premiums on categories of deposits that are not eligible for insurance. Accordingly, 43 countries levy charges against insured deposits. This trend is stronger among the newly introduced deposit insurance systems, where 65 percent of the newly introduced systems levy premiums on insured deposits.

A deposit insurance system that relies on an accumulated fund will need to charge premiums that are adequate to fund the system. The size of the premium needed to maintain a healthy fund will depend on the current condition of the banking system and its future prospects. Survey results show that premiums charged in 2003 ranged from a temporary zero percent of deposits for strong banks in the United States,[19] and a regular low of 0.05 percent in The Bahamas, Finland, and Lebanon to a high of 1.0 percent in Algeria, the Dominican Republic, Guatemala, and Macedonia, FYR (Statistical Appendix Table A5). The newer systems tended to have relatively high premiums, reflecting efforts to build the deposit insurance system fund.

Determining the adequacy of premiums requires detailed knowledge of the condition of each country's banking system and deposit insurance system. However, where information is available on both the target level of the fund and the size of the fund, only 37 percent of countries had a fully funded deposit insurance system. Moreover, in some cases, the fund was significantly below the targeted level.

Levying the premium only on insured deposits might be perceived as being both more equitable and more efficient. Banks that derive the greatest benefit from having insured deposits will also be required to contribute the most to the funding of the system. Similarly, institutions that specialize in "wholesale" funding, and hence that do not take insured deposits, will not be required to contribute to the system. Because banks select the composition of their liabilities on the basis of commercial criteria, the cost of deposit insurance will be a factor in their decision as to whether to be "wholesale" or "retail" funded; hence this funding arrangement might be regarded as producing more efficient outcomes. Applying premiums to insured deposits only, however, can be very difficult to implement and administer.

On the other hand, all banks gain from the public good of financial stability to which deposit insurance contributes, and, therefore, all should be expected to finance the deposit insurance system, irrespective of whether or not they directly benefit from it. This consideration suggests that premiums should be levied on all deposits. Levying the premium on all deposits is administratively much simpler and has the additional benefit of broadening the deposit insurance system's funding base.

Supplemental or Emergency Funding

The deposit insurance system's reserve fund can be jeopardized in the case of either an exceptionally large number of failures or the failure of a sufficiently large financial institution. Under these circumstances, claims may outstrip the available fund resources, irrespective of whether the deposit insurance system is structured as an ex post or an ex ante fund. To deal with this eventuality, a deposit insurance system is often structured to include supplemental or emergency sources of financial support in addition to its regular contributions or assessments. This supplemental funding generally takes one of two forms: (1) imposing a special levy on the contributing banks, and (2) borrowing.

Imposing an additional assessment on contributing banks may not generate the amount of funds needed, especially during a financial crisis. Furthermore, levying additional premiums runs the risk of exacerbating a financial crisis. Borrowing can provide more funds and generally falls into one of three categories (in order of preference): from the markets by issuing bonds (usually under a government guarantee), drawing on a line of credit from the government (usually the ministry of finance), or borrowing from commercial banks.

Borrowing by issuing bonds is preferred because it makes use of funds in the private sector rather than depleting government finances. Depending on the sophistication of the securities markets, however, it may be impractical to issue bonds, especially on a timely basis. Consequently, many countries make provisions for the government to assist a depleted fund with loans. Almost 60 percent of all explicit deposit insurance systems have access to such funding, as do almost 80 percent of the recently introduced systems, where information is available (Table 10). Borrowing from commercial banks is strictly discouraged because of the obvious conflict of interest of an insurer borrowing from an insured.

Some of the most important funding characteristics of recently introduced deposit insurance systems are provided in Table 10. With regard to the source of funding, most countries use joint arrangements, where the government provides part of the initial capital and/or back-up funding in case of an emergency. In general, developed countries tend to have systems that are primarily financed by the participating banks, whereas countries with low per capita income tend to rely on joint funding.

---

[19]By law, the FDIC in the United States does not impose premiums on the highest-quality banks when its fund is above its statutory target level of 1.25 percent of insured deposits, as it was in the year 2000.

Table 10. Most Important Characteristics of Recently Introduced Deposit Insurance Systems

Country	Funding Source[1]	Funding[2]	
		Risk adjustment	Government support
Albania	1	0	1
Algeria	1	1	...
Belarus	0	0	1
Bosnia and Herzegovina	0	0	0
Cyprus	0	0	1
Hong Kong SAR	0	1	1
Isle of Man	0	0	...
Jordan	1	0	0
Liechtenstein	0	0	...
Malta	0	0	0
Nicaragua	1	1	1
Paraguay	1	0	1
Russia	1	0	1
Serbia and Montenegro	1	0	1
Slovenia	1	0	1
Sudan	1	0	1
Turkmenistan	1	0	...
Zimbabwe	1	0	1

Sources: Statistical Tables A4 and A5.
[1] 0 = banks; 1 = joint.
[2] 0 = no; 1 = yes.

Accountability and Transparency

The Role of the Private Sector on the Deposit Insurance Agency Board

An important issue in the accountability of a deposit insurance agency concerns the extent to which the private sector should be involved in its governance. Because the deposit insurance fund is funded from premiums paid by the banking sector, it is sometimes argued that the banks should have a role in overseeing the way the fund is operated. Moreover, recent empirical research has emphasized the benefits of private involvement, arguing that it will contribute to peer monitoring and the soundness of the system. Although few systems are entirely run by the private sector (Germany provides one example), many more have banker representation on deposit insurance agency boards. However, to the extent that the board has access to commercially sensitive information, there is a clear risk of conflicts of interest for the private sector representatives. The greater the extent of the deposit insurance system's mandate, the greater these conflicts of interest can be expected to become. A possible solution is to establish a bankers' consultative committee distinct from the board. This will allow representatives of the private sector to be kept informed of, and to be consulted on, major policy changes while protecting the confidentiality of the deposit insurance system's operational work.

The share of deposit insurance systems mainly administered by representatives of government agencies has risen since 2000, from 56 percent to 63 percent (Table 11). The major reason for this change is the increasing tendency of new systems to heavily involve the central bank and other government agencies when establishing the fund, or even to locate it within an existing body. Statistical Appendix Table A8 summarizes the available information on whether the deposit insurance system is administered and/or managed inside or outside an existing public body (the central bank, a separate banking supervisor, or a ministerial body).

Public Transparency

Sound Practice: The efficiency and effectiveness of deposit insurance systems are enhanced by (1) describing their functions and powers by statute or contract; (2) stating explicitly the membership criteria and the degree of protection that the system does, and does not, offer; and (3) taking measures to promote public awareness of the existence of depositor protection.

Because deposit insurance systems exist to strengthen financial system soundness, the general public needs to be aware of the nature and extent to which they are protected by the system. They also, importantly, need to be aware of the limitations of deposit insurance system coverage, in particular of those institutions and products that are not covered by the system.

To promote the deposit insurance system's efficient and accountable discharge of its functions, it is preferable that its functions and powers be laid down in law, either by statute (where the system is public) or by contract (where the system is private). The deposit insurance law should also specify the types of instruments covered, the extent of coverage, and the conditions under which the commitment will be triggered, and should place a realistic time limit within which payouts are to be made. Other matters to be incorporated in the deposit insurance law will depend on the specific structure of the deposit insurance system adopted.

Second, membership conditions as well as the entry and exit criteria for the deposit insurance system should be clear and well understood. The public also needs to know which institutions are members of the system and which are not.

Finally, the deposit insurance system should be encouraged to publish, from time to time, a statement of its activities, and should promote public awareness of its tasks and responsibilities, as well as the level of protection that it makes available to depositors. Impor-

Table 11. Share of Regimes with Public, Joint, or Private Administration
(In percent)

Region	2000			2004		
	Public	Private	Joint	Public	Private	Joint
Africa	80	20	0	80	0	20
Asia	90	0	10	83	0	17
Europe	34	31	34	51	27	22
Middle East	50	0	50	50	0	50
Americas	76	12	12	84	11	5
Total	**56**	**21**	**23**	**63**	**12**	**21**

Source: Statistical Appendix Table A8.

tantly, this should also explain the nature and types of financial contract that are not subject to protection.

Public Awareness

Public awareness and education are important elements of a deposit insurance agency. Any government body that implements new or reform programs has a responsibility to actively promote public understanding by developing communications plans and a formal media and public relations structure. A deposit insurance system should articulate a message consistent with its mission and strategic plan. Publication of the benefits and limitations of the depositor protection system can help maintain the credibility of the deposit insurance system and enhance public confidence in the system.

As part of a transparent policy, a deposit insurance system can publicize the specifics of the deposit insurance system to the public and business community. This is crucial in winning and maintaining public confidence in the deposit insurance system and banking system, especially in an emerging market. Sound media and public relations programs will also promote understanding among the press, public, government, and banks. A deposit insurance system that lacks a communications plan will often spend much of its time on the defensive, reacting to criticism that may or may not be fair or accurate. This can result in a high stress level and an adverse impact on the credibility and effectiveness of the deposit insurance system.

The deposit insurance system can use press releases and public appearances by senior executives to announce positive developments regarding the key attributes of the deposit insurance system. This will help build long-standing relationships and trust with the media representatives who cover the deposit insurance system. Learning about the needs of the media will provide an opportunity to communicate the deposit insurance system perspective on events and issues. When this is included in news reports it will contribute to the public's confidence in the underlying strength of the deposit insurance system and the banking system.

These relationships will prove invaluable when the banking sector is experiencing problems. Prior to any bank failures, the deposit insurance system should develop a media and depositor education plan that answers, at a minimum, the following questions:
- Where will insured deposits be paid?
- Is there an acquiring bank to act as paying agent?
- Will all branch facilities be open for payment?
- When will deposits be paid?
- What information must an insured depositor provide to obtain payment?
- Must loans be repaid?

Providing this important information can help offset the troubling effects of bank closings. In these situations, it is vital for the deposit insurance agency to be proactive and quickly provide information, which can help build up or restore confidence in the banking system.

V Limiting Moral Hazard

Moral hazard and the weakening of market discipline are intrinsic to the existence of financial safety nets. In the specific case of a deposit insurance system, moral hazard arises because a risky institution does not have to pay higher interest costs on its deposits. In a competitive deposit market without insurance, riskier institutions would be able to attract deposits only by paying higher interest rates. The increased cost of funds would act as a market discipline, reducing banks' incentives toward excessive risk taking. However, once a deposit insurance system has been established, the existence of the deposit guarantee makes insured depositors less sensitive to risk. Hence, in designing a deposit insurance system, there are four mechanisms that can limit the potential distortions of moral hazard: limited scope and coverage, coinsurance, risk-adjusted insurance premiums, and subordinated debt.

Limited Scope and Coverage

Limiting the scope and coverage of a deposit insurance system is the most important technique to limit moral hazard. As discussed in Section IV, restricting deposit insurance system coverage to small-scale depositors will limit the impairment of risk-monitoring activities by creditors. Moreover, exclusion of deposits of "insiders" (that is, bank owners or managers or closely connected persons) will also limit the moral hazard implications. More generally, shareholders of failed banks must not be protected by the safety net, ensuring that the incentives for gambling for resurrection or adopting high-risk activities are not rewarded.

Coinsurance

Coinsurance (or the "deductible") is a technique frequently used to reduce moral hazard in the provision of commercial insurance. It involves the insured depositor bearing part of the risk of loss, in the sense that coverage is less than 100 percent of the value of the deposit. If the public policy objective is to preserve the stability of the financial system and, accordingly, coverage extends to more risk-sensitive depositors, coinsurance could apply to deposits of intermediate size and thereby play a useful role in containing moral hazard. However, coinsurance for depositors has a number of disadvantages. First, since it is virtually costless to transfer funds among banks, the prospect of *any* loss will presumably be sufficient to encourage a deposit run. Second, the main justification for creating a deposit insurance system on consumer protection grounds is that small depositors lack the information and incentives to be able to monitor the performance of banks. Given that the scope for small-scale depositors to exercise market discipline is already very limited, coinsurance can be expected to have at best a very limited impact on the incentives those small-scale depositors face.

Although recent econometric evidence suggests that coinsurance is indeed desirable, the share of countries using the technique declined slightly between 2000 and 2004, from 28 percent to 24 percent. Relatively few recently introduced deposit insurance systems coinsure deposits, and most of those that do belong to the upper part of the income distribution (for example, Cyprus, Isle of Man, and Malta). Most of these systems coinsure a certain part of the whole coverage limit, often 90 percent, as specified by the EU directive on deposit insurance. Albania decided to cover a first tranche (up to US$3,000) in full, and 85 percent of the next US$3,000.

Risk-Adjusted Insurance Premiums

Like coinsurance, the idea of risk-adjusted premiums is borrowed from the provision of commercial insurance: the greater the insurance risk, the greater the insurance premium. In a risk-related system of insurance premiums, banks pay a fee based on their relative risk of failure. This means that, in theory, banks that engage in riskier behavior would be subject to higher premiums. If the risk of failure is priced properly, the benefits of increased risk taking will be taxed away, limiting banks' incentive to engage in overly risky activities. This should in turn lead banks to limit their risk exposure and hence act to correct the erosion of market discipline resulting from the introduction of deposit insurance. Risk-adjusted deposit insurance premiums restore an element of market discipline, because riskier institutions are required to pay higher premiums than conservative ones. The second half of the 1990s saw a strong increase in the proportion of deposit insurance systems using risk-adjusted premiums, from 9 percent in 1995 to 35 percent in 2000.

Subordinated Debt

Although bank regulators have long permitted subordinated debt to form a component of banks' capital base, some economists have argued that there is a case for a mandatory requirement that banks issue subordinated debt as part of their capital structure. The case for mandatory subordinated debt rests on the premise that uninsured debt holders, unlike equity holders, do not receive the benefits of risks that turn out well, although they must bear the costs of risks that turn out bad enough that the equity holders are wiped out. Because the insolvency risk of holders of uninsured subordinated debt is the same as that of the deposit insurer, their incentives are therefore closely aligned, and both have strong incentives to monitor banks' activities. In effect, therefore, the interest rate on uninsured debt is like a risk-adjusted deposit insurance premium, but without any of the implementation problems discussed above.

Although attractive in principle, the subordinated debt proposal requires a number of market infrastructure elements that are lacking in many countries in the world. First, a country's securities markets must be deep enough to support the required levels of debt issuance, and liquid enough to generate prices from which meaningful information can be extracted. In addition, the price discovery process in markets must be free of manipulation, which calls for effective securities regulation. There must also be a class of nonbank financial institutions that would be the main investors in these instruments. A third precondition is that investors must believe their investments in subordinated debt are at risk. Even if these instruments are not covered by the deposit insurance system, if there is a widespread presumption that the authorities will intervene to protect nondeposit creditors, then the subordinated debt will not perform the market-signaling function as intended.

Statistical Appendix

Table A1. Deposit Insurance: Major Developments

Country	Major Developments
Africa	
Cameroon	In 1999, the six countries of the Central Bank of West African States (BEAC) decided to jointly establish a deposit insurance system (DIS). However, the scheme did not go into operation, because only two member countries (Cameroon and Chad) ratified the treaty.
Central African Rep.	In 1999, the six countries of the BEAC decided to jointly establish a DIS. However, the scheme did not go into operation, because only two member countries (Cameroon and Chad) ratified the treaty.
Chad	In 1999, the six countries of the BEAC decided to jointly establish a DIS. However, the scheme did not go into operation, because only two member countries (Cameroon and Chad) ratified the treaty.
Equatorial Guinea	In 1999, the six countries of the BEAC decided to jointly establish a DIS. However, the scheme did not go into operation, because only two member countries (Cameroon and Chad) ratified the treaty.
Gabon	In 1999, the six countries of the BEAC decided to jointly establish a DIS. However, the scheme did not go into operation, because only two member countries (Cameroon and Chad) ratified the treaty.
Kenya	There was an amendment to the Banking Act in 2001, clarifying the role and the powers of the DIS. However, the fund is still being criticized for its lack of transparency.
Nigeria	No significant changes.
Republic of Congo	In 1999, the six countries of the BEAC decided to jointly establish a DIS. However, the scheme did not go into operation, because only two member countries (Cameroon and Chad) ratified the treaty.
Sudan	Not included in Garcia (2000). Information is difficult to obtain.
Tanzania	No significant changes since 2000. The description of governance arrangements in Garcia (2000) was corrected.
Uganda	No significant changes since 2000. There are plans to reform the DIS, creating a deposit insurance agency (DIA) that has more autonomy from the central bank and participates in the process of handling bank failures, which were frequent in recent years.
Zimbabwe	A DIS was introduced in 2003. The responsibilities of the DIA are expected to broaden in the future.
Americas	
Argentina	After a temporary period without an explicit DIS, a specialized DIA was established in 1995 to cope with banking problems after the Mexican crisis. In response to the financial crisis in 2001, special arrangements were set in place, e.g., a deposit freeze, pesification of deposits, and an extension of coverage to Arg$30,000. In addition, a Banking Liquidity Fund was established in December 2001, entrusting its administration to the DIA in the capacity of a trustee.
The Bahamas	No indication of major changes.
Barbados	The legislation for the establishment of the DIS is still under way. The draft law was sent out to the banking industry for comments. The central bank and the ministry of finance (MOF) are currently reviewing these comments.
Bolivia	The law on the establishment of the "Fondo de Garantia de Depósitos" has not been enacted yet. It is unclear how legislation will proceed. There is a "Financial Restructuring Fund," officially protecting privileged claims (such as check deposits, savings and time deposits, trust deposits, and prepaid letters of credit), but without any specification of amounts. Banks must contribute quarterly an increasing share of their deposits: 0.015 percent in 2002, 0.045 percent in 2003, and so on, up to 0.125 percent beginning in 2005. Once a resolution process is triggered, resources are used along with resources from the central bank as defined in the Banking Law.

Table A1 *(continued)*

Country	Major Developments
Brazil	In 2002, Resolution 3024 of the National Monetary Council amended and consolidated the rules of the Statutes and Regulations of the Fundo Garantidor de Créditos.
Canada	There are multiple DIAs in Canada. In particular, regional agencies (like Régie de l'assurance-dépôts du Québec, recently reorganized and merged with other Autorité des marchés financiers players in Quebec) supplement the Canada Deposit Insurance Corporation (CDIC). The information herein is for the CDIC.
Chile	There is no funded system in Chile. The Banking Act establishes a state guarantee for time deposits and savings accounts. This guarantee shall only benefit individuals and shall cover 90 percent of the obligation's amount up to a limit of 120 unidades de fomento. In the case of obligations in sight deposits, the central bank shall provide the funds necessary to pay obligations. For such a purpose, the central bank shall acquire assets from the bank or grant loans to it.
Colombia	There are numerous changes relative to Garcia (2000). Most of them are present in the World Bank database as well as in CDIC (2002).
Costa Rica	There is an explicit and full constitutional guarantee for public banks. An explicit, limited scheme is under discussion for private banks, but the draft legislation has not been presented to congress. The constitutional guarantee on deposits at public banks has not been eliminated and there are no plans to do so.
Dominican Republic	The Dominican Republic introduced an explicit DIS for savings and loans associations and the National Housing Bank in 1962. A law giving broader protection in the form of legal priority passed the legislature in 1999, but was vetoed by the president. In November 2002, after one of the largest banks experienced large withdrawals of deposits, the authorities established an emergency fund (Fondo de Contingencia) within the central bank that governs payouts to depositors and the transfer of a failed institution to viable ones. However, several irregularities and a full bailout of large depositors took place.
Ecuador	A DIS was enacted in July 1998, but was soon overridden by a full guarantee that has been in place since December 1998. The DIA was supposed to operate the full guarantee and to conduct bank restructuring operations, mainly in the form of "purchase and assumption operations." Given the lack of fiscal funds, the Agency for Deposit Guarantees honored the blanket guarantee with central bank resources. The full guarantee was not rolled back, but depositors still suffered losses owing to the inability of the government to honor its full guarantee.
El Salvador	Before November 1999, the old Banks Law stated that banks should pay a fee to the central bank in order to create a fund to insure deposits. But this disposition was never applied. So after the failure of one medium financial institution and two small ones, the Bank Deposit Insurer was created. El Salvador implemented a new DIS in 1999, covering most deposits. In 2002, the responsibilities and rights of the DIA were extended to allow for additional participation in bank restructuring.
Guatemala	Selected aspects (fund target, premium rate, and coverage of foreign currency deposits) were changed during the past four years.
Honduras	In 2000, Honduras introduced a full state guarantee valid until 2002, which was extended several times. Currently the full guarantee is rolled back.
Jamaica	Jamaica instituted an explicit full guarantee in 1995. A limited DIS was enacted in March 1998 and began operations in September 1998.
Mexico	In 1999, the Bank Savings Protection Institute (IPAB) was established to assume the operations of Fondo Bancario de Protección al Ahorro, handle resolution procedures, and prepare the phasing out of the full guarantee. From 2003 onward, guaranteed obligations are being narrowed qualitatively and quantitatively. From 2005 onward, the limited DIS is fully operational.
Nicaragua	In 2001, an explicit limited scheme was introduced. However, the law dictated that there should be a full government guarantee for the first six months. This full guarantee was prolonged later (to 18 months). Officially it expired August 1, 2002.
Paraguay	In December 2003, the "Law on Deposit Guarantees and the Resolution of Financial Intermediaries" was passed. It is run by the central bank. The law also specifies resolution mechanisms in case of individual bank failures and systemic events. In particular, it envisages the implementation of a full guarantee in case of a systemic event.
Peru	There have been no significant legal changes since 2000. However, since 1999, the DIS has been actively involved in restructuring the banking sector. In 2000, emergency legislation was passed, allowing the DIS to operate a line of credit for fragile banks. The information on governance in Garcia (2000) was reevaluated. Even though a law in 1999 gave more flexibility to the deposit insurance fund, there are close links to the bank supervisor, which provides human resources, decides on premiums, and pays out reimbursements.

Table A1 *(continued)*

Country	Major Developments
Suriname	Deposits in the Postal Savings Bank are insured by the government. For all other banks, there is no explicit DIS.
Trinidad and Tobago	No significant changes since 2000.
United States	It is planned to merge the Bank Insurance Fund and the Savings Association Insurance Fund into the Deposit Insurance Fund.
Uruguay	No significant changes since 2000.
Venezuela	The coverage level was increased and annual premiums were decreased. Coverage was raised temporarily to 2 percent in 1994 to help fund the heavy assistance to troubled banks. During this episode, Venezuela selectively paid more than the legally stated limit on coverage. Moreover, the DIS, as the official liquidator of banks, was extensively involved in liquidation procedures. In 2001, the Law on Banks and Financial Institutions was changed with minor implications for the DIS. Currently, further changes are being discussed.
Asia	
Azerbaijan	A law is being drafted to create an independent compulsory DIS. It is supposed to cover current accounts of individuals up to US$200, term deposits in local currency up to US$6,000, and term deposits in foreign currency up to US$2,000. Premiums were planned to be equivalent to 0.5 percent of total deposits. Following the IMF suggestions, it was decided to postpone introduction of the DIS to after 2004. The chapter on deposit insurance was therefore deleted from the banking system law approved by parliament in January 2004, and a separate deposit insurance law is being prepared. The timing of parliamentary adoption of the law as well as the introduction of the DIS was expected before the second half of 2005.
Bangladesh	The Bank Deposit Insurance Act was changed in 2000. Besides smaller adjustments, the changes included an increase in coverage and the premium rate.
Hong Kong SAR	The Deposit Protection Scheme Ordinance was passed by the Legislative Council in 2004, and is expected to start in 2006. The information herein is based on the ordinance as well as on information provided by the Hong Kong Monetary Authority in the CDIC (2002) survey.
India	Since 2001, the DIS has had to settle claims for large amounts owing to the failure of banks, particularly in the cooperative sector, causing a drain on the DIS. Currently, Indian authorities are discussing a major reform of the DIS. The government has announced that, before proposing legislative changes, the U.S. Federal Deposit Insurance Corporation (FDIC) model should be closely studied and a suitable model evolved for India.
Indonesia	A full explicit guarantee was introduced in 1998. In line with phasing out the blanket guarantee program, a Deposit Insurance Company (DIC) was planned. Instead of the present unlimited guarantee for deposits, savings, and checking accounts, the new rules would cap coverage at a total of Rp 100 million (US$10,759) for each customer for all accounts at one bank. The policy will be implemented gradually and is scheduled to be completed within the next two and a half years. The law has to be signed by the president.
Japan	Initially, Japan had a coverage limit of US$71,000. Owing to continued pressure on banks, Japan extended full coverage as an emergency measure and postponed removal from April 2001 until April 2002. It was then decided to phase out full coverage. Term deposits have limited coverage up to ¥10 million since April 2002; all other major accounts were fully guaranteed until March 2005. Unlimited insurance will remain for settlement-use accounts.
Kazakhstan	A new regulation became effective in 2003. It extended coverage significantly (to deposits other than time deposits), excluded high-rate deposits, and changed terms and conditions of funding. Coinsurance was abandoned and premium system was changed from risk-based to flat.
Korea	After the introduction of an explicit scheme in 1996, the Korean deposit insurance fund experienced numerous changes. At the height of the crisis, Korea placed a temporary full guarantee on deposits. The segregated deposit insurance agencies of nonbank financial institutions were consolidated under the Korean DIC in 1998. In 2000/01, the blanket guarantee was revoked, but implicit guarantees seemed to remain for nonbank financial institutions, which continue to be a source of fragility.
Kyrgyz Republic	A draft law was presented to parliament in 2001. The World Bank and the IMF voiced their concerns and suggested that the government first strengthen the court system. In response, the MOF withdrew the law and drafted a new bankruptcy law for banks. A new draft law is being prepared. Coverage has been set at the equivalent of US$100 and certain deposits will not be covered.
Malaysia	A full guarantee was introduced in December 1997. It did not expire explicitly. Currently, an explicit limited scheme is under consideration.
Marshall Islands	Branches of U.S. commercial banks are insured by the FDIC, under special U.S. legislation.

Table A1 *(continued)*

Country	Major Developments
Micronesia	Commercial banks are insured by the FDIC, under special U.S. legislation.
Mongolia	A draft law was expected to be discussed in parliament in 2003. It would create an independent DIA with initial capitalization equivalent to US$70,000 coming from the central bank. The current draft provides for a flat premium of 1 percent of deposits to be paid by commercial banks (there is currently one state-owned bank in Mongolia, the Savings Bank, which collects roughly 40 percent of total deposits; that bank was privatized by the end of 2004) and for coverage of up to 90 percent of all deposits. However, amendments will be put forward to reduce both the level of premiums and the coverage.
Philippines	In May 2000, the General Banking Law was enacted, repealing the Philippine DIC power to conduct independent examination of banks. There are plans to make further amendments to the Deposit Insurance Law, including a significant increase in coverage levels. A new rating model was implemented.
Singapore	The introduction of a DIS is currently being considered. A second consultation paper was prepared by the Monetary Authority in April 2004.
Sri Lanka	No significant changes. It is still the case that none of the licensed commercial banks participate in the voluntary Deposit Insurance Scheme.
Taiwan Province of China	In 1999, membership in the DIS became mandatory and risk-adjusted premiums were introduced. After continuing pressure on banks, a "Financial Restructuring Fund" was established under the DIA, providing a blanket guarantee for all creditors and liquidity to problem institutions. The fund was established using money from the state budget and extensively participates in bank restructuring. Although the full guarantee was originally planned to be rolled back until July 2004, it is still in place.
Tajikistan	A law was presented to parliament in 2003. If the law is or has been approved, the central bank will put forward the funds needed to capitalize the fund. The fund will be independent and accountable to the central bank, will be allowed to invest exclusively in government and national bank securities, and will reimburse depositors only when bank liquidation has been initiated. The commercial banks will pay a quarterly flat premium equivalent to 0.05 percent of insured deposits. Coverage will be upgraded every year: in the first year, the fund will cover up to the equivalent of US$100; then US$200, US$400, and US$800.
Thailand	A blanket guarantee was issued in 1997. The responsibility for depositor payouts, liquidity support for banks, and related restructuring efforts was assigned to the Federal Institutions Development Fund (FDIF). Founded through an emergency decree in 1985, it is hosted within the central bank and receives funds from the government and from banks. Currently, the authorities are planning to replace the full guarantees by preparing a law on the introduction of a limited DIS.
Turkmenistan	A DIS was introduced in 2000. However, information is not available from public sources.
Uzbekistan	According to the International Association of Deposit Insurers (2003) there is a compulsory deposit insurance. Each private bank is required to pay an initial contribution equivalent to 0.1 percent of its equity and a quarterly contribution equivalent to 0.50 percent of the value of the deposits insured. The fund covers deposits of individuals and it will reimburse depositors when the bank's license is revoked.
Europe	
Albania	A DIS was introduced in 2002.
Austria	No indication of major changes.
Belarus	The current legislation is being reconsidered, owing to numerous problems caused by the current DIS. In particular, banks and deposits in local and foreign currencies are treated unequally. Several interest groups and ministries oppose the draft.
Belgium	No indication of major changes since 2000, but information is scarce.
Bosnia and Herzegovina	Enacted in 1998. First banks were admitted in 2001. The August 2002 law on deposit insurance established a new agency by merging the Federation Bosnia and Herzegovina Deposit Insurance Agency and Republika Srpska Deposit Insurance Agency, which was introduced in 2001. At that point, further banks were admitted to the scheme.
Bulgaria	No indication of major changes since 2000.
Croatia	The DIA is part of the Bank Restructuring Agency, which is independent de jure. Government officials are members of the deposit insurance agency board.
Cyprus	The DIS was set up in 2000 in line with the EU Directive on Deposit Guarantee Schemes.
Czech Republic	No indication of major changes since 2000.

Table A1 *(continued)*

Country	Major Developments
Denmark	In 2002, the Act on the Danish Guarantee Fund was consolidated and slightly changed.
Estonia	No indication of major changes since 2000, except for the coverage limit, which will increase gradually to reach EU levels in 2007.
Finland	No indication of major changes since 2000.
France	No indication of major changes since 2000.
Germany	Germany has both public and private schemes. There are separate private schemes for commercial banks, savings banks, giro institutions, and credit cooperatives. Since August 1998 an official compulsory scheme for commercial banks has been in place. The private scheme supplements the public scheme by covering the 10 percent deductible and topping up coverage. The private DIS can assist troubled banks.
Gibraltar	No indication of major changes since 2000. Information available concerning the exclusion of certain types of deposits contradicts Garcia (2000).
Greece	In 2000, legislation was changed. In particular, cooperative banks were included in the scheme.
Hungary	The law and several features of the Hungarian DIS (e.g., coverage and treatment of foreign bank branches) changed on May 1, 2004, the date of EU accession.
Iceland	A new act went into force in 2000. Guarantees under this act are entrusted to a special institute, the Depositors' and Investors' Guarantee Fund. The objective of the act is to guarantee a minimum level of protection to depositors in commercial and savings banks, and to customers of companies engaged in securities trading. This new protection scheme replaced the former deposit guarantee funds for commercial and savings banks.
Ireland	No indication of major changes since 2000, but information is scarce.
Isle of Man	Not included in Garcia (2000), although in operation since 2002.
Italy	Italy has two separate DIS systems, one for commercial banks (which have 90 percent of the system's deposits) and the other for smaller, mutual institutions.
Kosovo	Kosovo considered (and is considering) a DIS, but international organizations (including the IMF) discouraged it.
Latvia	In 2001, the administration of the DIS was transferred to the newly created Financial Services Authority, the Financial and Capital Markets Commission.
Liechtenstein	No indication of major changes since 2000.
Lithuania	In 2001, to harmonize elements of the Lithuanian deposit insurance with the requirements of the European Union, a new law was passed, expanding the deposit insurance coverage to deposits of companies. From then on, interest on deposits and other forms of banks' liabilities was also covered. In addition, credit unions were included in the scheme. In 2002, coverage was extended to liabilities to investors and the name was changed to "State Company Deposit and Investment Insurance."
Luxembourg	In 2003, the nonprofit association Association pour la Garantie des Dépôts, Luxembourg (Deposit Guarantee Association, Luxembourg, AGDL) was established. It privately manages the ex post DIS in Luxembourg and separately covers cash deposits and investment transactions.
Macedonia, FYR	There were frequent reorganizations and amendments to the law in recent years. In particular, the DIS is now run by a public body. In addition, certain deposits were excluded from coverage, coverage limits increased significantly, and the coinsurance scheme was adjusted.
Malta	A DIS was introduced in 2003.
Netherlands	Several changes are being considered, including the merger of the scheme for banks with the investor compensation scheme and the introduction of ex ante funding.
Norway	As of July 1, 2004, the Commercial Banks' Guarantee Fund and the Savings Banks Guarantee Fund were merged into one fund, the Norwegian Banks' Guarantee Fund.
Poland	During the past years, the compensation limit was gradually raised. In 2000 and 2001, laws and regulations were changed.
Portugal	Coinsurance was repealed in 1999.

Table A1 *(concluded)*

Country	Major Developments
Romania	Pursuant to the provisions of an emergency ordinance in 2001, the DIS was appointed as a rule to act as official receiver of insolvent banks. At present, the IMF is involved in the liquidation of several banks. Other changes include the inclusion of branches of foreign banks and a strong increase in the basic risk premium. There is a plan to insure deposits of corporations from 2005 onward.
Russia	In December 2003, a DIS for household deposits was adopted. It was subject to several exclusions (e.g., for the state-owned Sberbank, whose deposits will continue to be covered by a full state guarantee for several years) and an extensive screening process by the central bank that each bank has to undergo before being admitted. As a result, the scheme is not yet fully operational. In 2004, after the banking sector experienced renewed problems, a law was passed that governs central bank compensations for household deposits in banks not admitted to the scheme.
Serbia and Montenegro	Deposit insurance in Serbia was officially established in 1989, without being fully operational until 2001, when a wave of bank liquidations occurred. Since then, the DIA in Serbia and Montenegro has been involved in a series of bank liquidations. Currently, a new law is being discussed to tackle the low coverage and insufficient funds in the DIS, as well as fragmented and sometimes contradictory regulation.
Slovak Republic	The Deposit Protection Act was amended in 2001. In particular, coverage was extended to all natural persons (including entrepreneurs). In addition, the double level of deposit protection at building societies was removed. From 2004 on, upon accession to the EU, coverage has been extended to certain legal persons, and the coverage limit raised to €20,000.
Slovenia	An ex post scheme was introduced in 2001, in accordance with the EU directive. It is administered and managed by the central bank. In 2003, the coverage limit was raised to EU levels.
Spain	No significant changes since 1999, except for the coverage limit, which was raised to a level in accordance with EU standards.
Sweden	Sweden introduced a temporary guarantee for all bank liabilities in 1992, and replaced it with a formal system of deposit insurance to conform to EU standards in January 1996. Since 2000, no major changes to the DIS have been reported. However, the annual premium was significantly reduced, from 0.5 percent to 0.1 percent. Because the definition of eligible deposits is still not fully in line with the respective EU directive, further changes are being considered.
Switzerland	No change.
Turkey	Turkey has implicitly provided unlimited coverage since May 1994. An explicit, full state guarantee was enacted in December 1999. In 2000, administration and representation of the DIS was transferred to the bank supervisory authority. Currently, Turkey is in the transition phase to a limited guarantee. The practice of full insurance over savings deposits was officially removed as of July 5, 2004.
Ukraine	No significant changes since 2000.
United Kingdom	A new scheme was created under the Financial Services and Markets Act 2000 and became operational on December 1, 2001. It replaced a number of separate schemes and includes building societies and credit unions, which formerly had separate schemes.
Middle East	
Algeria	A DIS was introduced in 2003/04, just days before the failure of d'El Khalifa Bank.
Bahrain	No indication of major changes, even though Garcia (1999) mentions draft legislation to fund its system.
Israel	After several bank failures, the Bank of Israel proposed to introduce a DIS in 2002, which has not yet been enacted.
Jordan	Newly introduced in 2000.
Lebanon	No indication of significant changes.
Morocco	No information on significant changes during the past eight years.
Oman	No significant changes.
Tunisia	In 2001, a new law on banking activities was passed. It includes a provision to establish a guarantee mechanism for deposits that is compulsory for all banking institutions. The central bank is in charge of implementing the scheme and issuing regulations that govern its implementation.

Sources: Country authorities; and IMF staff.

Table A2. Deposit Insurance Agencies: General Characteristics

Country	Name of DIA	Type[1]	Blanket[2]	Enacted	Last Revised	Respon- sibilities[3]
Africa						
Kenya	Deposit Protection Fund Board Kenya	I	0	1985	2001	I
Nigeria	Nigeria Deposit Insurance Corporation	I	0	1989	...	I
Sudan	...	I	0	1996	...	...
Tanzania	Deposit Insurance Board, Bank of Tanzania	I	0	1994	...	I
Uganda	Bank of Uganda	I	0	1994	...	0
Zimbabwe	Deposit Protection Board of Zimbabwe	I	0	2003	...	0
Americas						
Argentina	Seguro de Depósitos Sociedad	I	0	1979	1995	I
The Bahamas	Deposit Insurance Corporation (The Bahamas)	I	0	1999	...	I
Brazil	Fundo Garantidor de Créditos	I	0	1974	2002	0
Canada	Canada Deposit Insurance Corporation	I	0	1976	1995	I
Chile	Banco Central de Chile	I	0	1986	...	...
Colombia	Fondo de Garantías de Instituciones Financieras	I	0	1985	1999	I
Dominican Republic	Fondo de Contingencia	I	0	1962	2002	I
Ecuador	Agencia de Garantía de Depósitos	I	I	1998	1999	I
El Salvador	Instituto de Garantía de Depósitos	I	0	1991	1999	I
Guatemala	Fondo para la Protección del Ahorro	I	0	1999	...	0
Honduras	Fondo de Seguros de Depósitos	I	I	1999	2003	I
Jamaica	Jamaica Deposit Insurance Corporation	I	0	1998	...	I
Mexico	Bank Savings Protection Institute	I	0	1986	1999	I
Nicaragua	Fondo de Garantía de Depósitos de las Instituciones Financieras (FOGADE)	I	0	2001	...	0
Paraguay	Fondo de Garantía de Depósitos (FGD)	I	0	2004	...	0
Peru	Fondo de Seguro de Depósitos	I	0	1992	1999	I
Trinidad and Tobago	Deposit Insurance Corporation (Trinidad and Tobago)	I	0	1986	...	I
United States	Federal Deposit Insurance Corporation (FDIC)	I	0	1934	1991	I
Venezuela	FOGADE	I	0	1985	2001	I
Asia						
Bangladesh	Deposit Insurance Trust Fund (Bangladesh Bank)	I	0	1984	2000	0
Hong Kong SAR	Hong Kong Deposit Protection Board	I	0	2006	...	0
India	Deposit Insurance and Credit Guarantee Corporation	I	0	1961	...	0
Indonesia	Indonesian Deposit Insurance Corporation	I	0	2005	2005	I
Japan	Deposit Insurance Corporation of Japan	I	0	1971	2002	I
Kazakhstan	Kazakhstan Deposit Guaranteeing (Insurance) Fund	I	0	1999	2003	0
Korea	Korea Deposit Insurance Corporation	I	0	1996	2001	I
Marshall Islands	FDIC	I	0	1975	...	I
Micronesia	FDIC	I	0	1963	...	I
Philippines	Philippine Deposit Insurance Corporation	I	0	1963	1992	I
Sri Lanka	Central Bank of Sri Lanka, Bank Supervision Department	I	0	1987	...	0
Taiwan Province of China	Central Deposit Insurance Corporation	I	I	1985	...	I
Thailand	Financial Institutions Development Fund	I	I	1985	1997	I
Turkmenistan	...	I	0	2000	...	...
Vietnam	Deposit Insurance of Vietnam	I	0	1999	2005	I
Europe						
Albania	Albanian Guarantee Agency	I	0	2002	...	0
Austria	Multiple schemes	I	0	1979	1996	I
Belarus	Guarantee Fund for the Protection of Deposits	I	0	1998	2001	I
Belgium	Fund for the Protection of Deposits and Financial Instruments	I	0	1974	1995	I
Bosnia and Herzegovina	Deposit Insurance Agency of the Federation of Bosnia and Herzegovina	I	0	1998	2002	I

Table A2 *(concluded)*

Country	Name of DIA	Type[1]	Blanket[2]	Enacted	Last Revised	Respon-sibilities[3]
Bulgaria	Deposit Insurance Fund—Bulgaria	1	0	1998	...	0
Croatia	State Agency for Deposit Insurance and Bank Rehabilitation	1	0	1997	1999	1
Cyprus	Deposit Protection Fund—Central Bank of Cyprus	1	0	2000	...	0
Czech Republic	Czech Deposit Insurance Fund	1	0	1994	...	0
Denmark	The Danish Guarantee Fund for Depositors and Investors	1	0	1988	1998	0
Estonia	Guarantee Fund	1	0	1998	2002	1
Finland	The Deposit Guarantee Fund Finland	1	0	1969	1999	0
France	Fonds de Garantie des Dépôts	1	0	1980	1999	0
Germany	Entschaedigungseinrichtigung Deutscher Banken	1	0	1966	1998	0
Gibraltar	Gibraltar Deposit Insurance Board	1	0	1998	...	0
Greece	Hellenic Deposit Guarantee Fund	1	0	1993	2000	0
Hungary	National Deposit Insurance Fund of Hungary	1	0	1993	2004	1
Iceland	Depositors' and Investors' Guarantee Fund (Iceland)	1	0	1985	2000	0
Ireland	Central Bank of Ireland	1	0	1989	1995	1
Isle of Man	Financial Supervision Commission	1	0	1991	...	1
Italy	Fondo Interbancario di tutela dei Depositi	1	0	1987	1999	1
Latvia	Financial and Capital Market Commission	1	0	1998	2001	1
Lithuania	State Company Deposit and Investment Insurance	1	0	1996	2002	1
Luxembourg	AGDL	1	0	1989	2003	0
Macedonia, FYR	Deposit Insurance Fund Skopje	1	0	1996	2003	0
Malta	Malta Financial Services Authority	1	0	2003	...	0
Netherlands	Deposit Guarantee Scheme	1	0	1979	1998	0
Norway	Norwegian Banks' Guarantee Fund	1	0	1961	2004	1
Poland	Bank Guarantee Fund	1	0	1995	2001	1
Portugal	Fundo de Garantia de Depositos	1	0	1992	1999	0
Romania	Bank Deposit Guarantee Fund Romania	1	0	1996	2001	0
Russia	Russian Deposit Insurance Agency	1	0	2003	2004	1
Serbia and Montenegro	Agency for Deposit Insurance, Bank Rehabilitation, Bankruptcy and Liquidation	1	0	1989	2001	1
Slovak Republic	Deposit Protection Fund of the Slovak Republic	1	0	1996	2004	0
Slovenia	Bank of Slovenia	1	0	2001		1
Spain	FGD	1	0	1977	1996	1
Sweden	Deposit Guarantee Board Sweden	1	0	1996	...	0
Switzerland	Swiss Bankers Association	1	0	1984	1993	0
Turkey	Savings Deposit Insurance Fund, Banking Regulation and Supervision Agency	1	1	1983	2000	1
Ukraine	Deposit Guarantee Fund of Ukraine	1	0	1998	...	0
United Kingdom	Financial Services Compensation Scheme	1	0	1982	2001	0
Middle East						
Algeria	Société de Garantie des Dépôts Bancaires	1	0	2004	...	0
Bahrain	Deposit Protection Scheme Board, Bahrain Monetary Agency	1	0	1993	...	0
Jordan	Deposit Insurance Corporation Jordan	1	0	2000		1
Lebanon	National Deposit Guarantee Institution	1	0	1967	1991	0
Morocco	Collective Guarantee Deposit Fund	1	0	1993	1996	1
Oman	Central Bank of Oman	1	0	1995	...	1

Sources: Country authorities, and IMF staff.

[1]Explicit = 1; implicit = 0

[2]No = 0; yes = 1.

[3]Broad = 1; narrow = 0.

Table A3. Membership in Explicit Limited Deposit Insurance Systems

Country	Institutional Membership	Compulsory[1]	Branches of Foreign Banks[2]	Number of Member Institutions
Africa				
Kenya	Every institution (e.g., banks, other financial institutions, mortgage finance companies) that is licensed to conduct business in Kenya.	1	1	51
Nigeria	Licensed deposit-taking financial institutions.	1	1	90
Sudan	...	0	...	...
Tanzania	All licensed banks, including the Tanzania Postal Bank, and financial institutions that take deposits.	1	1	28
Uganda	Banks and credit institutions.	1	0	25
Zimbabwe	Commercial banks, building societies, merchant banks, finance and discount houses.	1	1	39
Americas				
Argentina	All institutions providing financial intermediation licensed by the central bank, savings banks, and credit unions, if they are supervised.	1	1	102
The Bahamas	Every licensed bank conducting business in Bahamian currency.	1	1	13
Brazil	All financial institutions as well as savings and loan associations that operate in Brazil—except for credit cooperatives and their credit sections.	1	1	273
Canada	All retail deposit-taking institutions. Banks and trust or loan companies.	1	1	858
Chile	Commercial and savings banks of all types, but not credit cooperatives.	...	1	26
Colombia	All entities that take deposits, including banks, finance companies, savings associations, leasing companies, and investment trusts. Separate scheme for credit cooperatives.	1	1	108
Dominican Republic	Savings and loan associations, commercial banks, development banks, mortgage banks, and other institutions. The National Housing Bank, Banco Agricola Corporacion de Fomento Industrial, and certain cooperative institutions are excluded.	1	1	~200
Ecuador	Commercial banks, savings banks, and credit cooperatives, if they are supervised.	1	1	...
El Salvador	All banks, except one state-owned bank and credit cooperatives.	1	1	12
Guatemala	Private domestic banks and branches of foreign banks.	1	1	20
Honduras	Private banks, savings and loan associations, finance companies, and foreign banks authorized to accept deposits.	1	1	14
Jamaica	All financial institutions licensed to accept deposits.	1	1	19
Mexico	Full-service banking institutions (commercial banks), but not savings or credit cooperatives.	1	1	50
Nicaragua	All financial institutions that are licensed to take deposits.	1	1	9
Paraguay	Private banks authorized to operate in Paraguay.	1	1	30
Peru	All commercial banks and certain other financial institutions that are supervised and authorized to accept deposits, including municipal and rural savings and credit unions.	1	1	42
Trinidad and Tobago	All licensed financial institutions, including commercial banks, finance houses, trust companies, and merchant banks.	1	1	~20

Table A3 *(continued)*

Country	Institutional Membership	Compulsory[1]	Branches of Foreign Banks[2]	Number of Member Institutions
United States	All depository institutions that accept retail deposits. Savings associations and credit unions are insured by separate schemes.	I	I	9,400
Venezuela	Banks, including mortgage banks, development banks, savings and loan entities, municipal credit institutions and other financial institutions licensed in Venezuela.	I	...	~60
Asia				
Bangladesh	All scheduled private, foreign, and Islamic financial institutions.	I	I	~50
Hong Kong SAR	Licensed banks. Restricted licensed banks and deposit-taking companies are excluded from membership because they are not permitted to take small deposits.	I	I	146
India	Commercial, cooperative, and rural banks that are either publicly or privately owned.	I	I	...
Indonesia	All banks (commercial and rural), but not Village Credit Organizations.	I	I	131
Japan	Commercial, trust, long-term credit, and *shinkin* banks; credit cooperatives; and labor credit associations. A separate scheme covers agricultural and credit cooperatives. Government-related institutions and branches of foreign banks are not covered.	I	0	658
Kazakhstan	Banks that are licensed to accept deposits and that have met international prudential standards.	I	I	21
Korea	Banks, securities, insurance companies, merchant banks, mutual savings and finance companies, and credit unions.	I	I	1,590
Marshall Islands	Branches of U.S. commercial banks. Membership for the single domestic bank is under consideration.	0	I	3
Micronesia	Commercial banks.	0	I	...
Philippines	All deposit-taking institutions, including commercial banks, savings banks, mortgage banks, rural banks, development banks, cooperative banks, stock savings and loan associations, and branches and agencies in the Philippines of foreign banks.	I	I	926
Sri Lanka	Registered banking institutions and cooperative societies carrying on banking business. However, none of the licensed commercial banks participate in the voluntary DIS. A new, separate, cross-guarantee scheme for cooperative societies was initiated in 1999.	0	2	...
Taiwan Province of China	All financial institutions licensed to accept deposits or trust funds.	I	I	294
Europe				
Albania	All entities granted a banking license.	I	I	14
Austria	Credit institutions that take deposits.	I	I	~850
Belarus	There are three groups of banks. Two large banks do not pay insurance premiums and are covered by an implicit guarantee.	I	...	~30
Belgium	All credit institutions governed by Belgian law and Belgian branches of non-EU incorporated banks.	I	I	~85
Bosnia and Herzegovina	All banks.	I	I	23
Bulgaria	All banks legally licensed to take deposits.	I	I	32
Croatia	Commercial and savings banks, but not savings and loans associations.	I	I	...

Table A3 *(continued)*

Country	Institutional Membership	Compulsory[1]	Branches of Foreign Banks[2]	Number of Member Institutions
Cyprus	All domestic banks operating in the Republic of Cyprus (including branches of foreign banks) are members of the scheme. Cooperative credit institutions participate in an equivalent deposit protection scheme.	I	I	11
Czech Republic	All licensed banks (including banks and building societies) and the branches and agencies of foreign banks. Branches of foreign banks may opt out if their home country scheme offers equivalent coverage.	I	I	36
Denmark	Commercial, savings, and cooperative banks, and the branches of foreign banks. Mortgage banks and investment companies.	I	I	227
Estonia	Credit and investment institutions and mandatory pension funds.	I	I	30
Finland	All deposit banks: commercial banks, savings banks, savings banks with limited liability, cooperative banks, and local cooperative banks.	I	2	335
France	All licensed credit institutions.	I	I	949
Germany	The official DIS covers all licensed banking institutions. In addition, there are separate private schemes for commercial banks, savings banks, and credit cooperatives.	I	2	2,500
Gibraltar	Banks incorporated in Gibraltar, offices from banks from non–European Economic Area (EEA) countries that are authorized to operate in Gibraltar.	I	I	11
Greece	All credit institutions authorized to conduct banking business in Greece, except for the Postal Savings Bank and the Deposit and Loan Fund. Since 2000, cooperative banks are included in the scheme.	I	I	45
Hungary	All credit institutions operating in Hungary, including savings cooperatives, home savings banks, and credit cooperatives.	I	I	231
Iceland	Until January 2000, Iceland had two separate deposit insurance systems—one for commercial banks and the other for savings banks. They have now been combined.	I	I	40
Ireland	All authorized credit institutions, including building societies.	I	I	...
Isle of Man	Banks.	I	I	50
Italy	There are two separate deposit insurance systems: the Interbank Fund for Protection of Deposits, comprising all Italian banks except for mutual banks and the Mutual Bank Depositor Guarantee Fund for mutual banks.	I	I	305
Latvia	All banks authorized to accept deposits from natural persons.	I	I	...
Lithuania	Commercial banks, credit unions, and branches of foreign banks.	I	I	64
Luxembourg	All institutions licensed to accept deposits and investment firms.	I	I	...
Macedonia, FYR	Banks and savings houses established in the former Yugoslav Republic of Macedonia.	I	0	33
Malta	All financial intermediaries and banks.	I	I	...
Netherlands	All financial institutions licensed to take deposits.	I	I	...

Table A3 *(concluded)*

Country	Institutional Membership	Compulsory[1]	Branches of Foreign Banks[2]	Number of Member Institutions
Norway	Commercial banks and savings banks.	1	1	~200
Poland	All commercial and cooperative banks operating in Poland, including foreign bank branches.	1	1	660
Portugal	Credit institutions that have their head office in Portugal and are authorized to take deposits and branches of non-EU banks.	1	1	53
Romania	Banks and branches of foreign banks licensed to operate in Romania.	1	1	34
Russia	All banks taking retail deposits of physical persons and admitted to the scheme after an extensive screening process by the central bank.	1	1	...
Serbia and Montenegro	All banks and other depository institutions.	1		45
Slovak Republic	Commercial banks and building societies.	1	1	20
Slovenia	All deposit-taking institutions (banks, savings banks) with authorization of the Bank of Slovenia. Credit cooperatives (savings and loan undertakings) are not covered.	1	1	23
Spain	All Spanish credit institutions included in the Register of Banks. There are three separate schemes: one for commercial banks, one for savings banks, and one for credit cooperatives.	1	1	244
Sweden	All Swedish and foreign commercial banks and all investment firms that are licensed to accept deposits.	1	1	140
Switzerland	All banks operating in Switzerland, i.e., members of the Swiss Bankers Association.	0	1	...
Turkey	Deposit-taking banks. A group of financial institutions called "Special Finance Houses" operate a separate scheme.	1	1	38
Ukraine	Licensed commercial banks that are included in the National Bank of Ukraine's Register of Banks. The Savings Bank of Ukraine is not a member.	1	1	...
United Kingdom	U.K. incorporated banks licensed to take deposits, non-EEA incorporated banks that are authorized to take deposits through U.K. offices, and branches of U.K. incorporated banks in the EEA. Building societies and credit unions are also covered.	1	1	450
Middle East				
Algeria	All banks, including branches of foreign banks.	1	1	~20
Bahrain	Offices of full commercial banks.	1	1	~120
Jordan	All deposit-taking institutions with the exception of Islamic banks, unless anyone of them decides to join the insurance system.	1	1	19
Lebanon	All banks existing and operating in Lebanon.	1	1	...
Morocco	"All credit institutions receiving public funds."	1	0	~50
Oman	Banks licensed by the central bank to accept deposits and operating in Oman.	1	...	...

Sources: Country authorities; and IMF staff.

[1]Compulsory = 1; voluntary = 0.

[2]No = 0; yes = 1; voluntary = 2.

Table A4. Private and Official Funding for Explicit Limited Deposit Insurance Systems

Country	Fund[1]	Source[2]	Has Private Funding[3]	Sources of Additional Funding/ Official Backing	Invested Fund Resources	Legal Priority for Depositor or the Deposit Insurance System[3]
Africa						
Kenya	I	I	I	Deposit insurance system can borrow from central bank and banks, receive subventions and donations.	Money placed in an account with the central bank to be invested by the board in treasury bills, treasury bonds or other securities issued by the government.	0
Nigeria	I	I	I	Government (the ministry of finance and central bank) provided initial capital, and can make loans or directly provide funds. In addition, the deposit insurance system can borrow or levy special contributions from members.	Federal government securities.	I
Sudan	I	I	I	...	...	...
Tanzania	I	I	I	The government provided initial capital and the central bank can make loans.	Tanzanian T-bills and loans to banks.	0
Uganda	I	I	I	Government provided initial capital. The deposit insurance system can borrow from the central bank and from the government.	T-bills.	I
Zimbabwe	I	I	I	Deposit insurance system is allowed to borrow from the government, through the central bank, in the event of an urgent liquidity need.	T-bills and other liquid and low-risk securities.	I
Americas						
Argentina	I	I	I	Access to financial markets and borrowing from banks. Central bank contributed a small share of initial capital.	By law, fund resources should be invested under similar conditions as those established for the investment of international reserves.	I
The Bahamas	I	I	I	Ability to borrow.	Investments limited to government securities.	I
Brazil	I	0	I	Anticipated assessment of member contributions for up to 24 months. Through previous understanding between the Central Bank of Brazil and the fund administrators, additional funding can be arranged.	Brazilian government bonds.	0
Canada	I	I	I	Fund can borrow from markets or government, but is charged private market rates.	The CDIC Act does not set out specific criteria for the use of the deposit insurance fund.	0
Chile	0	2	0	...	...	I

Table A4 *(continued)*

Country	Fund[1]	Source[2]	Has Private Funding[3]	Sources of Additional Funding/ Official Backing	Invested Fund Resources	Legal Priority for Depositor or the Deposit Insurance System[3]
Colombia	1	0	1	It is understood that the state is the ultimate guarantor. The deposit insurance agency has authority to obtain loans from domestic and foreign institutions or any other source authorized by its board of directors.	Colombian government securities.	1
Dominican Republic	1	1	1	The government and the central bank will provide funds and the central bank can lend on short notice.	Short-term securities issued by supranational organizations or by governments, and overnight deposits.	1
Ecuador	1	1	1	Until December 1999, the fund could request that the central bank provide liquidity to a bank in rehabilitation. The deposit insurance system also received government bonds from the ministry of finance. However, under the dollarization scheme, no new money can be created. Because the deposit insurance system has run out of cash, deposits have been frozen since March 1999, and must be repaid by government bonds.	Deposit insurance system uses the same criteria as for investing international reserves.	1
El Salvador	1	1	1	The central bank provided initial funding. In case of insufficient funding, the deposit insurance system can borrow from the central bank or from other financial institutions.	Securities at home and abroad, foreign bank deposits, taking into account risk and liquidity.	0
Guatemala	1	1	1	The government may cover the deficit of the fund or increase its coverage. It may make a temporary, exceptional contribution, which is to be repaid by the banks later.	Foreign or domestic government bonds or central bank securities, but no investments in participating banks.	1
Honduras	1	1	1	The government made an initial contribution, which may be repaid over time. The central bank has a contingent credit line for the deposit insurance system; the ministry of finance may issue bonds.	A special fund at the central bank.	0
Jamaica	1	1	1	The fund can borrow in the markets or from the government and has an explicit government guarantee.	Jamaican or foreign government securities or banks.	0

Table A4 *(continued)*

Country	Fund[1]	Source[2]	Has Private Funding[3]	Sources of Additional Funding/ Official Backing	Invested Fund Resources	Legal Priority for Depositor or the Deposit Insurance System[3]
Mexico	I	I	I	Fund has access to financial markets and government funding. In the past, it has borrowed extensively from the central bank and the ministry of finance.	Liquid government securities or deposits of the central bank.	I
Nicaragua	I	I	I	The deposit insurance system can borrow with a government guarantee.	The funds are administered by the central bank, and invested according to the rules specified for international reserves.	...
Paraguay	I	I	I	Government provided initial capital; additional government funding when needed.	Central bank decides on investments, taking into account risk, liquidity, and revenue.	I
Peru	I	I	I	The central bank and the treasury made initial contributions. Fund may borrow from the treasury (using credit lines from the treasury approved by urgency degree) and from financial markets.	Investments include corporate, foreign currency, and government securities. Peruvian finance companies are excluded.	0
Trinidad and Tobago	I	I	I	Central bank made an initial contribution, matches banks' special contributions in case of insufficient funds, and may lend to the fund.	Cash and the marketable securities of domestic or foreign governments.	I
United States	I	I	I	The government provided initial capital, bore savings and loan losses, and can lend.	Special issue of U.S. government securities.	I
Venezuela	I	I	I	Central bank and government have borne losses and have refinanced the deposit insurance system after losses during the 1994 crises. The central bank may make advances in case of funding needs.	Securities that are liquid and profitable, equity interests.	I
Asia						
Bangladesh	I	I	I	Interest on assets, lending from central bank.	Approved, risk-free securities and investments.	I
Hong Kong SAR	I	0	I	The deposit insurance system may borrow (by decision of the management committee), when the need arises.	Broad investment and hedging opportunities, but approval by the financial secretary is necessary.	...
India	I	I	I	The central bank provided initial capital. Central bank and government give support with parliamentary approval.	Indian central government securities.	0
Indonesia	I	I	I	The government provided initial capital. Agency can borrow from the government and from central bank.	Indonesian government securities and central bank instruments.	I

Table A4 *(continued)*

Country	Fund[1]	Source[2]	Has Private Funding[3]	Sources of Additional Funding/ Official Backing	Invested Fund Resources	Legal Priority for Depositor or the Deposit Insurance System[3]
Japan	I	I	I	Government and central bank provided initial capital. The central bank makes loans. The government has provided substantial assistance. It is possible to finance the scheme through borrowing from private financial institutions with guarantee by the government.	Central and local government securities and corporate bonds.	0
Kazakhstan	I	I	I	The deposit insurance system can borrow from the government and the central bank.	Government securities.	I
Korea	I	I	I	The Korean Deposit Insurance Corporation is legally authorized to issue bonds and borrow from the government or central bank with ministry of finance approval. In recent years, the government has injected large amounts of resources.	1. Purchase of government bonds and public loans, or other securities designated by the committee. 2. Deposit in insured financial institutions designated by the committee. 3. Other methods prescribed by the ministry of finance.	0
Marshall Islands	I	0	I	Deposits are insured by the U.S. FDIC.	Special issue of U.S. government securities.	I
Micronesia	I	0	I	Deposits are insured by the U.S. FDIC.	Special issue of U.S. government securities.	I
Philippines	I	I	I	The government provided initial capital, and can borrow from the central bank and from markets.	Obligations of the government or obligations guaranteed by the government.	0
Sri Lanka	I	I	I	The central bank provided initial capital and has advanced funds.	. . .	0
Taiwan Province of China	I	I	I	The government provided initial capital. The central bank makes loans against collateral or a guarantee from the ministry of finance. In 2001, the Financial Restructuring Fund was established, using money from the state budget.	Cash, securities, government bonds, and bank debentures.	0
Turkmenistan	I	. . .	I	. . .	. . .	. . .
Vietnam	I	I	I	The government provided initial capital. The fund can borrow from the government.	. . .	I

Table A4 *(continued)*

Country	Fund[1]	Source[2]	Has Private Funding[3]	Sources of Additional Funding/ Official Backing	Invested Fund Resources	Legal Priority for Depositor or the Deposit Insurance System[3]
Europe						
Albania	I	I	I	To the extent that the amount required for compensating insured deposits exceeds the available financial resources of the agency, funds from the state budget shall be made available to the agency. Initial funding from the state budget (capital of about $3.5 million).	Albanian T-bills.	0
Austria	0	I	I	Issue of government-guaranteed bonds in case of insufficient funds.	. . .	I
Belarus	I	0	I	There is a system of explicit and implicit guarantees, the latter being provided by the government and the central bank.	Resources are recorded in the accounts of the central bank and invested according to central bank policy on asset transactions.	I
Belgium	I	I	I	The state has provided a limited temporary guarantee. Premium can be raised by a maximum of 0.04 percent if fund's liquid assets fall below a critical value.	. . .	0
Bosnia and Herzegovina	I	0	I	No.	Only securities guaranteed by EU countries.	0
Bulgaria	I	0	I	Initial (entry) premiums from banks, additional contributions from banks, borrowing from markets, and, as a last resort, from the government. Loans drawn by the fund may be secured by a guarantee issued by the government, or by fund's assets, including fund's future claims on banks for annual premium contributions.	Government securities issued or guaranteed by the government; short-term deposits with commercial banks that are authorized dealers of government securities; deposits with the Bulgarian National Bank.	I
Croatia	I	I	I	The fund may borrow from the central bank.	Short-term government and central bank securities.	I
Cyprus	I	0	I	The deposit insurance system may borrow (by decision of the management committee) on the guarantee of the members of the fund, when the need arises.	Treasury bills or other government securities in Cyprus pounds or equivalent foreign securities with a maximum remaining maturity of 12 months.	0
Czech Republic	I	I	I	The government and the central bank would equally make loans to cover any shortfall in funding. In addition, deposit insurance system has access to financial markets.	The board approved eligible instruments in 2002 (government bonds, domestic bonds, foreign bonds guaranteed by EU governments rated A3 or better).	0

Table A4 *(continued)*

Country	Fund[1]	Source[2]	Has Private Funding[3]	Sources of Additional Funding/ Official Backing	Invested Fund Resources	Legal Priority for Depositor or the Deposit Insurance System[3]
Denmark	I	I	I	Deposit insurance system can borrow from banks with a guarantee from the government. Further contributions of banks.	Danish government bonds with a maturity of less than five years and cash balances with the central bank.	0
Estonia	I	I	I	The government made an initial contribution. The fund can borrow without a government guarantee or ask the government to borrow a limited amount on its behalf, or apply for a state loan or a state guarantee for a loan taken by the fund.	Organization for Economic Cooperation and Development country bonds and deposits of nonmember credit institutions.	0
Finland	I	I	I	The government and the central bank have borne losses. The fund can borrow with a government guarantee. Member banks are obliged to grant loans in case funds are not sufficient.	Safe and profitable investments safeguarding the liquidity of the fund as well as in compliance with the principle of deconcentrating risks. The assets may not be invested in the bank belonging to the fund.	0
France	I	0	0	The government recapitalized Credit Lyonnais outside the deposit insurance system. Both the old and the new deposit insurance system are funded solely from private sources.	Funds are invested principally in debt securities or in unit trusts whose assets are mainly composed of debt securities, issued by "highly reputable" issuers, the list of which shall be established by the cash management committee of the guarantee fund.	0
Germany	I	0	0	Local governments have supported the scheme for savings institutions. Other schemes can borrow, but the law requires that compensation under the public scheme be paid from members' annual supplementary contributions.	The funds are with KfW, a public bank.	0
Gibraltar	0	0	I	No official backing.	...	0
Greece	I	I	I	60 percent of the start-up funding was provided by the central bank. The new law requires the member banks to pay additional contributions up to a certain limit when regular funds are not sufficient. In addition, the fund can raise loans.	80 percent in members' certificates of deposit, 20 percent in government paper.	0
Hungary	I	I	I	The government will guarantee fund borrowing from the central bank or private markets if requested.	Hungarian government bonds, credit institution deposits.	I
Iceland	I	0	I	No support.	...	0

Table A4 *(continued)*

Country	Fund[1]	Source[2]	Has Private Funding[3]	Sources of Additional Funding/ Official Backing	Invested Fund Resources	Legal Priority for Depositor or the Deposit Insurance System[3]
Ireland	I	0	0	...	Funds collected from the credit institutions are held in interest-bearing deposit accounts at the Central Bank of Ireland.	0
Isle of Man	0	0	I		...	0
Italy	0	I	I	Under the Legge Decree, the Bank of Italy can make low-interest-rate loans to facilitate a large payout. The government has recently provided substantial financial assistance to the deposit insurance system.	...	I
Latvia	I	I	I	The Bank of Latvia and the government made initial contributions. Compensation is paid from the government's budget if fund resources are inadequate.	Latvian government securities.	I
Lithuania	I	I	I	Access to financial markets. The possibilities of additional government funding were confined in the new law. The government provided initial capital and will cover any shortfall with loans.	Only in securities of the Lithuanian government.	I
Luxembourg	0	0	0	...	...	...
Macedonia, FYR	I	I	I	The central bank and the government can extend credit if the fund lacks resources to pay insured depositors.	Securities issued by the central bank or the government of the former Yugoslav Republic of Macedonia. The fund is also allowed to invest in certain debt securities issued by foreign countries.	I
Malta	I	0	I	Borrowing from financial markets and additional contributions from members.	...	...
Netherlands	0	I	I	The central bank provides interest-free bridge financing and backstop financing.	...	0
Norway	I	I	I	During the banking crisis, the government created a Government Bank Insurance Fund to make loans to the Commercial Bank and the Savings Bank Guarantee Funds, whose resources had been depleted by the banking crisis.	...	I

Table A4 *(continued)*

Country	Fund[1]	Source[2]	Has Private Funding[3]	Sources of Additional Funding/ Official Backing	Invested Fund Resources	Legal Priority for Depositor or the Deposit Insurance System[3]
Poland	I	I	I	The Bank of Poland and the government contributed initial capital. The central bank can make loans to the deposit insurance system. The deposit insurance system can also receive subsidies from the state budget.	Treasury securities.	I
Portugal	I	I	I	The Bank of Portugal provided initial capital. By law, the central bank can grant financial resources the fund requires to meet its Immediate needs. Access to financial markets.	Assets agreed on with the central bank.	0
Romania	I	I	I	The fund can borrow from the state, the central bank, and other sources. The government can guarantee funds raised on financial markets.	Romanian T-bills.	0
Russia	I	I	I	Part of the initial capital was paid in by the Agency for the Restructuring of Credit Organizations. The fund can receive state support ex post.	Specified by law in Article 38.3.	…
Serbia and Montenegro	I	I	I	Bonds issued by the agency, and federal budget funds.	DIA may invest its unallocated cash through banks and purchase short-term securities on money market.	…
Slovak Republic	I	I	I	The central bank made an initial contribution. It can also lend to the deposit insurance system.	The fund's liquid assets are kept in a special account at the National Bank of Slovakia. The fund may purchase government securities with a maturity of up to one year from the date of purchase.	0
Slovenia	0	0	I	Temporary access to central bank funds.	…	I
Spain	I	I	I	To safeguard the stability of member institutions as a whole, the central bank can make limited loans.	Interest-bearing account at the National Debt Office. Investments must take the form of national debt or other highly liquid, low-risk assets.	0
Sweden	I	I	I	The government has borne losses. The deposit insurance system may borrow from the National Debt Office.	Interest-bearing account at the National Debt Office.	0
Switzerland	0	0	I	No. The Swiss Bankers Association borrows under normal market conditions.	…	I
Turkey	I	I	I	Credit may be extended by the central bank or the treasury in case of insufficiency in funding.	The fund's assets are placed in banks, according to an internal investment directive.	I

Table A4 *(concluded)*

Country	Fund[1]	Source[2]	Has Private Funding[3]	Sources of Additional Funding/ Official Backing	Invested Fund Resources	Legal Priority for Depositor or the Deposit Insurance System[3]
Ukraine	I	I	I	The government made an initial contribution through the National Bank of the Ukraine. Deposit insurance system can borrow from the government and requires special charges from banks.	Ukrainian government securities.	I
United Kingdom	0	0	0	There is no public funding for the deposit insurance system, but it may borrow limited amounts in the markets with treasury approval.	Treasury bills.	I
Middle East						
Algeria	I	I	I	...	...	...
Bahrain	0	0	I	No. If funds do not suffice, payments are made on a pro rata basis.	...	0
Jordan	I	I	I	The government contributed one-third of initial capital. The fund can raise the premium in case its reserves fall below a certain target level. In case of emergency, the corporation may borrow directly or it may issue debenture bonds to meet its obligations. The law contains an explicit provision that rules out further government involvement.	Investments are confined to government bonds, bonds guaranteed by the government, and deposits with the central bank of Jordan.	I
Lebanon	I	I	I	The central bank contributed half of the deposit insurance system initial capital. The government matches banks' annual contributions. If the fund is depleted, the central bank replenishes it by making interest-free loans.	Lebanese T-bills, bonds, and real estate in Lebanon.	...
Morocco	I	0	I	No public support was used to establish the deposit insurance system and nonpublic monies are provided for in the legislation.	Negotiable securities of the Moroccan government.	0
Oman	I	I	I	The central bank matched half of the member banks' initial contributions; the fund can borrow from the government, the central bank, and member banks.	Investments must take into account risk, liquidity, and revenue.	I

Sources: Country authorities; and IMF staff.
[1]Ex ante = 1; ex post = 0.
[2]Private = 0; joint = 1; public = 2.
[3]No = 0; yes = 1.

Table A5. Building the Fund in an Explicit Limited Deposit Insurance System

Country	Fund Target (In percent of deposits)	Actual Funds (In percent of deposits/ assets)	Premium Base[1]	Annual Premiums	Risk-Adjusted Premiums (In percent of assessment base)[2]	Basis for Risk Adjustment	Description
Africa							
Kenya	20.00	1.60	0	0.15	0	...	
Nigeria	No	...	0	0.94	0	...	
Sudan	...	0.20	...	...	...	...	
Tanzania	3.00	1.00	0	0.10	0	...	
Uganda	Yes	Deficit	0	0.20	0	...	
Zimbabwe	1.00	15.00	1	0.74	0	...	
Americas							
Argentina	5.00	0.36	0	0.015	1	Formula that includes provisions, capital adequacy ratio (CAR), CAMEL, and risk assets.	Normally premiums are assessed as a flat rate, but central bank can establish an additional risk premium as a function of several risk indicators. The normal monthly premium can vary between 0.015 and 0.06 of the monthly average of daily balances of deposits.
The Bahamas	20–25 million	...	1	0.05	0	...	Central bank provided half of the system's initial capital.
Brazil	5.00	0.04	1	0.30	0	...	
Canada	No	0.14	1	[0.02, 0.04, 0.08, 0.16]	1	Quantitative and qualitative factors, including CAR, profitability, asset concentration, regulatory rating, and adherence to standards.	The law in Canada does not require the CDIC to accumulate a fund. Instead, it sets aside provisions to cover expected future losses and accumulates them in a reserve (typically called an allowance for loan losses (ALL)). Currently, the CDIC has resources exceeding the ALL.
Chile	...	...	...	...	...	...	Government is responsible for time and savings deposits, the central bank for demand deposits.
Colombia	5.00	5.00	0	0.50	1	CAMEL system.	Differential premiums are assessed on the basis of a CAMEL system. Risk adjustment is applied ex post, through a refund (since 2000). Until 1998, base rate was 0.15 percent; from 1998 to 2000 it was 0.6 percent; in 2002 it was changed to 0.5 percent. In 2007 it will be lowered to 0.3 percent.
Dominican Republic	5.00	Deficit	0	1.00	0	...	The premium originally specified in the law was 0.1 percent. Owing to increasing funding needs, it was raised to 1 percent in 2003.
Ecuador	50.00	Deficit	0	0.65	1	Risk rating developed by the deposit insurance agency.	Special conditions owing to crisis situation.

Table A5 (continued)

Country	Fund Target (In percent of deposits)	Actual Funds (In percent of deposits/ assets)	Premium Base[1]	Annual Premiums	Risk-Adjusted Premiums (In percent of assessment base)[2]	Basis for Risk Adjustment	Description
El Salvador	>1.00	0.53	1	0.1–0.45	1	If the bank has substandard securities or is subject to intervention or special supervision.	Premium can be raised from 0.1 to 0.3 to repay debt. If the bank has substandard securities or is subject to intervention or special supervision, a risk-based markup of 50 percent is applied.
Guatemala	5.00	4.00	1	1.00	0	...	
Honduras	5.00	0.43	1	≤0.25	0	...	
Jamaica	1.00	...	1	0.15	0	...	
Mexico	No	0.10	Liabilities subject to ordinary fee contributions, including off-balance-sheet liabilities, less financing received from other financial intermediaries.	0.40	0	...	In principle, the law allows for differential premiums. However, a system for assigning risk levels does not exist yet though there are plans to introduce risk-based premiums.
Nicaragua	...	0.20	0	0.75+ra	1	Risk assessment by international rating agencies.	
Paraguay	10.00	New scheme	1	0.36	0	...	
Peru	No	1.90	1	0.45–1.45	1	Several supervisory criteria are applied, including CAR.	There are differential premiums for five different risk categories. The premium applies only to deposits of individuals and nonprofit institutions. Currently the premiums are 0.45, 0.6, 0.95, 1.25, and 1.45.
Trinidad and Tobago	No	1.32	0	0.20	0	...	
United States	1.25	1.32	0	0.0–0.27	1	Capital and CAMELS ratios	www.fdic.gov/deposit/insurance/risk/rrps_ovr.html
Venezuela	...	4.00	1	0.50	0	...	
Asia							
Bangladesh	...	0.38	0	0.07	0	...	Deposit insurance agency finances were separated from those of the central bank. Deposit insurance agency is now able to borrow from the central bank.
Hong Kong SAR	...	...	...	...	1	Supervisory ratings	

Table A5 *(continued)*

Country	Fund Target (In percent of deposits)	Actual Funds (In percent of deposits/ assets)	Premium Base[1]	Annual Premiums	Risk-Adjusted Premiums (In percent of assessment base)[2]	Basis for Risk Adjustment	Description
India	No	0.10	I	0.08	0	...	Since 2001, the deposit insurance system has had to settle claims for large amounts. For this reason, the DIA has, with central bank approval, decided to increase the premium from 0.05 percent of assessable deposits to 0.08 percent for the financial year 2004–05, and to 0.1 for the financial year 2005–06.
Indonesia	2.50	...	0	0.10	0	...	Risk-weighted premiums are allowed but not required.
Japan	No	In deficit	I	0.08	0	...	There are two premium rates. One is for deposits for settlement (0.09 percent) and another for other deposits (0.08 percent). The effective rate in early 2006 was 0.084 percent.
Kazakhstan	Yes	2.20	I	0.16–0.25	0	...	During the first two years of membership, the premium rate is 0.25 percent of insurable deposits; in subsequent years it is 0.16 percent.
Korea	...	0.10	I	0.10	0	...	
Marshall Islands	1.25	1.32	0	0.0–0.27	I	Capital and CAMELS ratios.	www.fdic.gov/deposit/insurance/risk/rrps_ovr.html
Micronesia	1.25	1.32	0	0.0–0.27	I	Capital and CAMELS ratios.	www.fdic.gov/deposit/insurance/risk/rrps_ovr.html
Philippines	No	1.58	0	0.20	0	...	
Sri Lanka	...	Very low	0	0.15	0	...	
Taiwan Province of China	5.00	0.15	I	0.05 to 0.06	I	Nine categories reflecting CAR and rating on the early warning system.	At present, premium rates are based on three different levels of risk, namely, 0.05 percent, 0.055 percent, and 0.06 percent of covered deposits, using a CAMEL-like system. Each of the three indicators applied is subdivided into three levels, with the result that each insured institution may be assigned to any one of nine different risk groups.
Thailand	2.0 percent of insured deposits	1.00					
Turkmenistan	...	New scheme	...	...	0	...	
Vietnam			Total deposits of individuals	0.15	0	...	

Table A5 *(continued)*

Country	Fund Target (In percent of deposits)	Actual Funds (In percent of deposits/ assets)	Premium Base[1]	Annual Premiums	Risk-Adjusted Premiums (In percent of assessment base)[2]	Basis for Risk Adjustment	Description
Europe							
Albania	5.00	0.45	I	0.50	0	. . .	Annual premium for deposit insurance is calculated at 0.5 percent of the arithmetic average of the amount of the insured deposits recorded in the bank after each business day during the last quarter of the preceding year.
Austria	. . .	. . .	I	Pro rata, ex post	0	. . .	Private, ex-post scheme; government-guaranteed bonds may be issued.
Belarus	In preparation	7.10	I	. . .	0	. . .	Some banks do not have to pay premiums; some a premium of 1.2 percent; and some a premium depending on the ratio of deposits to capital.
Belgium	0.50	0.25	I	0.175	I	. . .	
Bosnia and Herzegovina	7.50	0.60	0	0.30	0	. . .	
Bulgaria	5.00	2.00	I	0.50	0	. . .	
Croatia	5.00	0.85	I	0.125	I	As determined by the central bank.	
Cyprus	CP 2 million	0.01	0	. . .	0	. . .	The deposit insurance system uses a mixture of ex post and ex ante funding. Banks have to provide initial capital over the first years of operation, and have to provide special and supplementary contributions whenever funds fall below the basic capital of 2 million Cyprus pounds or whenever it appears to the committee that there is a possibility that payments may exhaust the accumulated resources.
Czech Republic	No	0.40	I	0.10	0	. . .	
Denmark	0.04	0.17	I	0.00–0.20	0	. . .	Deposit insurance system can borrow from banks with a guarantee from the government.
Estonia	3.00	0.70	I	0.28	0	. . .	The annual premium has decreased steadily since 2001.
Finland	2.00	0.30	I	0.05	I	Solvency ratio.	

Table A5 (continued)

Country	Fund Target (In percent of deposits)	Actual Funds (In percent of deposits/ assets)	Premium Base[1]	Annual Premiums	Risk-Adjusted Premiums (In percent of assessment base)[2]	Basis for Risk Adjustment	Description
France	Yes	...	Deposit base adjusted for risk indicators	...	1	Banking supervisor calculates the adjustment based on CAMEL-like ratings.	Each member's contribution shall be equal, for each installment, to the product of the variable overall amount of the installment and the net share of risk attributed to it for such installment. A member's net share of risk is the ratio between its net risk amount and the sum of all members' net risk amounts.
Germany	3.00	3.00	Insured deposits	0.008 (statutory scheme) 0.01 (private scheme)	1	Risk category and length of membership in the private deposit insurance system.	
Gibraltar	No	...	1	...	0	...	Fund for administrative expenses and ex post contributions.
Greece	"A reasonable level"	0.27	0	0.0025–0.125	0	...	The calculation of annual contributions is based on a regressive scale. Above a certain threshold, the percentage premium rate is lowered. The scale's thresholds are revised each year by the board so that the ratio of total annual contributions to total deposits used for the calculation remains unchanged at the level of the first year of the agency's operation.
Hungary	1.50	1.20	1	[0.005, 0.05] +[rp]	1	Additional charge if bank falls below minimum CAR.	The base premiums decrease with size and are adjusted every year, taking into account funding needs and individual banks risks. In 2003, the base premium for the smallest banks was 0.05 percent for the largest 0.005.
Iceland	1.00	1.00	1	0.15	0	...	
Ireland	...	0.20	1	0.20	0	...	
Isle of Man	...	...	0	...	0	...	Funding is ex post. In case of a funding need, the levy on individual participants a year is the greater of £25,000 or 0.125 percent of its deposit base, subject to a maximum contribution of £250,000 a year.
Italy	0.40–0.80	0.40	1	...	1	Index with 28 gradations based on risk, solvency, maturity transformation, and performance.	
Latvia	...	0.10	1	0.20	0	...	

Table A5 (continued)

Country	Fund Target (In percent of deposits)	Actual Funds (In percent of deposits/ assets)	Premium Base[1]	Annual Premiums	Risk-Adjusted Premiums (In percent of assessment base)[2]	Basis for Risk Adjustment	Description
Lithuania	4.00	3.00	1	0.45	0	. . .	When the ratio between the fund's capital and all the deposits subject to insurance becomes higher than 4 percent. In this case the rate of the insurance premium for banks and foreign branches must not be lower than 0.001 percent, and for the credit unions not lower than 0.0005 percent.
Luxembourg	. . .	. . .	1	. . .	0	. . .	
Macedonia, FYR	5.00	2.00	0	1	0	. . .	In principle, the premium can be risk-adjusted, ranging from 1 to 5 percent, plus a supplement, if needed. Currently, there is a flat rate in place.
Malta	Lm 3 million	New scheme	0	0.10	0	. . .	The management committee may specify different rates or amounts of contributions or different bases for the calculation of contributions for different classes or categories of credit institutions.
Netherlands	. . .	. . .	Case by case	Case by case	0	. . .	In the Netherlands, the ex post assessments are made case by case on the basis of several items of data recently reported to the central bank. A comparison is made between the portfolios of the failed bank and the assessed bank. Costs are apportioned after consultation with the bankers' committee.
Norway	>1.50	>1.50	Risk-weighted assets and total deposits	0.005 percent of assets 0.01 percent of deposits	1	Assets that enter the assessment base are risk weighted.	
Poland	0.40	1.80	The assessment base is calculated using information on selected deposits and on- and off-balance-sheet assets, some of them adjusted for risk.	0.40	0	Some of the assets are subject to risk weighting.	Poland uses a combination of ex post and ex ante funding. The contributions for ex ante funding within the "guaranteed means protection fund" stay with banks until they are needed. Banks invest these funds in treasury securities and keep the interest. Premiums are not allowed to exceed 0.4 percent of deposits.

Table A5 *(continued)*

Country	Fund Target (In percent of deposits)	Actual Funds (In percent of deposits/ assets)	Premium Base[1]	Annual Premiums	Risk-Adjusted Premiums (In percent of assessment base)[2]	Basis for Risk Adjustment	Description
Portugal	No	0.84	I	0.05+ra	I	Solvency ratio	The basic rate ranges between 0.1 percent and 0.2 percent (except in special cases to be determined by the Banco de Portugal). The current base premium rate is 0.05 percent. Premiums take into account individual factors based on the average solvency ratio of each institution.
Romania	10.00	1.80	I	0.80+ra	0	Largely discretionary decision by the board of directors.	Information on risk adjustment is contradictory.
Russia	5.00	New scheme	I	0.20–1.20	0	. . .	The agency's board will set the quarterly premium, which cannot exceed 0.15 percent, except in special circumstances, when it could be raised to 0.3 percent for up to 18 months. As soon as the fund has accumulated the equivalent of 5 percent of insured deposits, the maximum premium will fall from 0.15 to 0.05.
Serbia and Montenegro	20.00	0.84	I	0.10	0	. . .	
Slovak Republic	1.50	0.47	I	0.10–0.75	0	. . .	
Slovenia	. . .	. . .	I	Ex post scheme	0	. . .	In case of a funding need, each bank contributes the amount calculated on the basis of its share in guaranteed deposits, subject to a limit of 3.2 percent of the assessment base. To secure liquidity in case of a funding need, there is an obligation to invest in first-rate, short-term securities in the amount equal to 2.5 percent of guaranteed deposits.
Spain	I.00	0.74/0.85	Deposits covered plus 5 percent of the quoted value of the stock covered by the system	0.00/40.06/0.10	0	. . .	Annual contributions shall be 0.2 percent of the deposits, but the ministry of economy is entitled to reduce the premium if the resources of one of the funds are declared enough to accomplish its purposes. At the moment the premium rates are 0.06 percent for banking institutions, 0.04 percent for saving banks, and 0.1 percent for credit cooperative banks.
Sweden	2.50	3.00	I	0.50	I	CAR.	A weight ranging from 0.6 to 1.4 is applied to the base rate of 0.1. The function determining the weight includes the CAR.
Switzerland	. . .	. . .	Discretion	Ex post	I	Based on earnings and some discretion.	

Table A5 *(concluded)*

Country	Fund Target (In percent of deposits)	Actual Funds (In percent of deposits/ assets)	Premium Base[1]	Annual Premiums	Risk-Adjusted Premiums (In percent of assessment base)[2]	Basis for Risk Adjustment	Description
Turkey	No	Deficit	Total savings deposits	0.125–0.235	1	CAR and loan quality.	The basic premium rate is 12.5 basis points (including foreign exchange and gold savings deposits). Risk-adjustment parameters include, among others, 2 basis points when the CAR is between 8 percent and 12 percent; 5 basis points when the CAR is below 8 percent; 1 basis point for banks with high unconsolidated foreign exchange positions; 3 basis points for banks with a high share of loans extended to related parties.
Ukraine	...	10.00	0	0.50	0	...	
United Kingdom	£5–£6 million	<£3 million	1	<0.30	0	...	The deposit insurance system operates on a pay-as-you-go basis. Levies are raised to cover the projected costs of the scheme, including compensation costs. The levy for the latter is made up of past compensations together with any compensations that can reasonably be anticipated for the next 12 months. The maximum levy is 0.3 percent of protected deposits.
Middle East							
Algeria	...	...	0	1.00	1	...	...
Bahrain	...	...	0	Ex post	0	...	
Jordan	3.00	1.03	0	0.25	0	...	
Lebanon	...	1.40	Credit accounts	0.05	0	...	In Lebanon, the premium paid by the banks is matched by a contribution from the government.
Morocco	No	0.80	0	0.20	0	...	
Oman	...	0.50	0	0.02	0	...	

Sources: Country authorities; and IMF staff.
[1]Total deposits = 0; insured deposits = 1; and others (specified).
[2]Yes = 1; no = 0.

Table A6. Deposit Coverage in Explicit Limited Deposit Insurance Systems

Country	Coverage (In U.S. dollars)	Coverage Limit (Domestic currency)	Coverage Ratio of 2003 GDP Per Capita	Types of Deposits Eligible	Coinsurance (Above threshold of)[1]	Description
Africa						
Kenya	1,309	100,000	3.01	All	0	
Nigeria	382	50,000	0.95	Most, including savings and checking accounts, annuity contracts, guaranteed investment certificates, traveler's checks, money orders, foreign currency deposits, and interbank deposits. Deposits that serve as collateral for a loan are excluded.	0	
Sudan	575	150,000	1.10	. . .	0	
Tanzania	240	250,000	0.89	Most, including savings and checking accounts, annuity contracts, certificates of deposit, guaranteed investment certificates, traveler's checks, money orders, certified drafts of checks, and foreign currency deposits.	0	
Uganda	1,593	3,000,000	6.43	Most	0	
Zimbabwe	301	200,000	0.47	Demand, savings, and time deposits as well as class B and class C shares. Negotiable CDs, bankers' acceptances, and foreign currency deposits are excluded.	0	
Americas						
Argentina	10,345	30,000	3.05	Most, including savings accounts, checking accounts, annuity contracts, and foreign currency deposits; and excluding those that pay more than 200 basis points above reference rate.	0	Any deposit made at a rate higher than a reference rate is not covered. The reference rate in force for each type of transaction is communicated beforehand by the Banco Central de la República Argentina.
The Bahamas	50,000	50,000	3.00	All. Savings accounts, checking accounts, CDs, guaranteed investment certificates, traveler's checks, money orders, certified drafts of checks.	0	
Brazil	6,541	20,000	2.28	Demand deposits, savings account deposits, time deposits (with or without the issuing of a certificate), bills of exchange, real estate bills, mortgage bills, real estate credit bills.	0	
Canada	42,825	60,000	1.24	Most. Savings and demand deposits and term deposits, such as guaranteed investment certificates and debentures issued by loan companies; money orders, drafts, and checks; traveler's checks.	0	Coverage is extended separately for retirement accounts and deposits held in trusts, which are additionally insured up to Can$60,000.
Chile	2,603	1,800,000	0.57	Savings accounts, checking accounts, CDs, money orders, and foreign currency deposits.	1	Demand deposits are insured in full by the central bank. Household savings and time deposits are coinsured 90 percent by the government to UF 120 (about US$3,400) a person a year.
Colombia	6,950	20,000,000	3.72	Most. Savings accounts, checking accounts, annuity contracts, CDs, and others.	1	Coinsurance on all insured accounts. Coinsurance 75 percent of Col$20 million and Col$15 million flat on larger accounts.

Table A6 *(continued)*

Country	Coverage (In U.S. dollars)	Coverage Limit (Domestic currency)	Coverage Ratio of 2003 GDP Per Capita	Types of Deposits Eligible	Coinsurance (Above threshold of)[1]	Description
Dominican Republic	15,952	500,000	8.74	Priority claims, as defined by the law: Deposits of the private sector (including sight deposits and savings accounts) and other instruments specified by law.	0	The scheme provides funds only up to a limited share of senior liabilities and up to 500,000 units of local currency per depositor. If the funds needed to pay out depositors up to the coverage level exceed 30 percent of these senior liabilities, payouts are calculated on a pro rata basis. The coverage limit is indexed to inflation.
Ecuador	500,000	500,000	252.39	Ecuador's DIS is normally confined to household deposits. It also does not cover the deposits of owners, current or recent directors, or managers or deposits that pay more than 3 percent above the average rate. The DIS covers offshore deposits.	0	Special conditions owing to crisis situation.
El Salvador	7,060	61,775	3.59	Most, excluding interbank deposits.	0	
Guatemala	1,989	20,000	1.33	Savings deposits, in home and in foreign currency.	0	
Honduras	9,514	165,000	9.75	Demand, savings, and term deposits held in national or foreign currency. Deposits that carry significantly higher rates or are illegal are excluded.	0	
Jamaica	5,392	300,000	1.82	Most, including savings accounts, checking accounts, CDs, money orders, certified drafts of checks, and foreign currency deposits (paid in Jamaica dollars).	0	
Mexico	136,269	400,000	94.77	Most, including savings accounts, checking accounts, CDs, traveler's checks, money orders, certified drafts of checks, and foreign currency deposits.	0	The full guarantee enacted in 1995 phases out gradually. In 2003, the coverage limit was 10 million Unidad de Invesion (UDIs); in 2004, 5 million UDIs. From 2005 on, it will be 400,000 UDIs. There is no coinsurance.
Nicaragua	20,000	20,000	41.95	Deposits of natural and legal persons, including foreign currency deposits. Illegal and high-rate deposits are excluded.	0	
Paraguay	9,086	58,663,950	9.27	Most, including foreign currency deposits. Criminal deposits are excluded.	0	
Peru	19,357	67,750	9.08	Demand deposits (for households and corporations) and a wide range of deposits (except bearer certificates) for natural persons, including CDs and foreign currency deposits.	0	
Trinidad and Tobago	8,052	50,000	1.03	Demand, savings, and time deposits. Foreign currency deposits are excluded.	0	
United States	100,000	100,000	2.80	All domestic, including savings accounts, checking accounts, CDs, traveler's checks, money orders, certified drafts of checks, and foreign currency deposits. Deposits booked offshore are not covered.	0	

Table A6 (*continued*)

Country	Coverage (In U.S. dollars)	Coverage Limit (Domestic currency)	Coverage Ratio of 2003 GDP Per Capita	Types of Deposits Eligible	Coinsurance (Above threshold of)[1]	Description
Venezuela	6,216	10,000,000	1.86	Most, including savings and checking accounts, fixed term deposits, savings certificates, term CDs, and unsecured bonds and investments in money market funds or liquid asset funds. Foreign currency deposits are excluded.	0	
Asia						
Bangladesh	1,702	100,000	4.64	Household deposits only.	0	In the new Deposit Insurance Act of 2000, provisions for the exclusion of certain types of deposits or depositors are missing.
Hong Kong SAR	12,842	100,000	0.56	Savings and checking accounts.	0	
India	2,148	100,000	3.99	India insures deposits in commercial, cooperative, and rural banks, except CDs.	0	
Indonesia	10,046	100,000,000	10.54	Current accounts, term deposits, CDs, and savings accounts.	0	
Japan	86,256	10,000,000	2.56	Most, including liquid deposits (ordinary savings, current deposits, and miscellaneous account) and other deposits (time deposits, installment savings, loan trusts, and bank debentures).	0	Owing to continued pressure on banks, Japan extended full coverage as an emergency measure and postponed removal from April 2001 until April 2002. Since April 2002 the coverage returned to ¥10 million. Deposits for settlement and payment purposes receive full guarantee.
Kazakhstan	2,673	400,000	1.36	Coverage includes conditional and demand deposits, current account balances, and card account balances, in local as well as in foreign currencies.	0	Coverage was significantly extended in 2003.
Korea	41,960	50,000,000	3.36	Deposits, savings, installments, secondary bills, and principal-covered trusts.	0	The laws and regulations were frequently amended in recent years. In particular, the temporary full guarantee that was introduced in 1997 ended in 2000. Since 2001, there has been a coverage limit of W50 million.
Marshall Islands	100,000	100,000	68.97	All	0	
Micronesia	100,000	100,000	50.00	All	0	
Philippines	4,500	250,000	1.89	Most, including savings and checking accounts, time and foreign currency deposits.	0	
Sri Lanka	1,370	100,000	1.49	. . .	0	
Taiwan Province of China	29,041	1,000,000	2.32	Most, including demand, savings, postal savings, and time deposits; trust funds whose uses are not designated by the trustees; and other deposits that the MOF has approved. Foreign currency deposits and negotiable CDs are excluded.	0	
Turkmenistan	. . .	. . .	. . .	. . .	0	

Table A6 (continued)

Country	Coverage (In U.S. dollars)	Coverage Limit (Domestic currency)	Coverage Ratio of 2003 GDP Per Capita	Types of Deposits Eligible	Coinsurance (Above threshold of)[1]	Description
Vietnam	3,140	50,000,000	6.72	Individual deposits	0	Coverage was increased from D30,000 in 2005.
Europe						
Albania	5,662	700,000	2.91	Deposits of individuals, in particular term deposits, demand deposits, and CDs. Nonnominative deposits (bearer securities) are excluded.	US$3,000	Up to US$3,000—100 percent. From $3,000 to $6,000—100 percent of $3,000 and 85 percent of the remaining portion.
Austria	22,614	20,000	0.73	Broad coverage: bank deposits, selected securities accounts; insider and criminal deposits excluded.	1	Coverage for nonhousehold deposits is limited to 90 percent of guaranteed deposit.
Belarus	1,000	1,000	0.51	Differential treatment for deposits in domestic and in foreign currency.	0	Coverage is different for different groups of banks and for different currencies.
Belgium	22,614	20,000	0.75	Belgium covers deposits, banknotes, bonds, and other claims on banks of households and small and medium-sized nonfinancial companies.	0	
Bosnia and Herzegovina	2,891	5,000	1.59	Most	0	
Bulgaria	7,532	15,000	3.58	Deposits in local and in foreign currency.	0	In contrast to Garcia's assessment, there is no coinsurance.
Croatia	12,022	100,000	2.37	Savings deposits. The term "savings deposits" applies to money of natural persons in kuna or foreign currency held on the account on the basis of a contract relating to a money deposit or as a deposit with a savings bank book.	0	
Cyprus	22,614	20,000	1.36	Savings account, checking account, and certified drafts of checks.	1	Compensation amounts to 90 percent of each protected deposit up to a maximum of the equivalent in Cyprus pounds of €20,000.
Czech Republic	28,267	25,000	3.38	Savings account, checking account, CDs, and foreign currency deposits.	1	Coinsurance on all covered accounts; 90 percent up to coverage limit.
Denmark	45,540	300,000	1.16	Most (registered deposits with the institutions mentioned and others).	0	DIS covers registered deposits for an amount of up to DKr 300,000. Certain categories are covered in full (personal pension accounts, establishment accounts, attorneys' client accounts, and other accounts established according to law).
Estonia	7,213	100,000	1.21	Excluding deposits of insiders, money launderers, government at all levels, large businesses, financial institutions including insurance companies, other members of the same corporate group, and those that pay substantially higher rates.	1	Coinsurance on all covered accounts; coinsurance is 90 percent of the coverage limit, which will increase gradually until 2007.
Finland	28,267	150,000	0.91	Savings accounts, checking accounts, and foreign currency deposits.	0	
France	79,148	70,000	2.77	Any credit balance deriving from normal banking transactions. Includes guarantee deposits, interest-bearing notes, payment media, and cash deposits.	0	

Table A6 *(continued)*

Country	Coverage (In U.S. dollars)	Coverage Limit (Domestic currency)	Coverage Ratio of 2003 GDP Per Capita	Types of Deposits Eligible	Coinsurance (Above threshold of)[1]	Description
Germany	22,614	20,000	0.77	Most. Statutory scheme excludes deposits that receive exceptionally high interest rates. The private scheme covers the deposits of nonbank creditors (both resident and nonresident) that are held in Germany and abroad, regardless of currency denomination.	1	The official scheme offers 90 percent coinsurance to €20,000, but the deductible is covered by private schemes. The private scheme offers coverage to 30 percent of the bank's capital. The private schemes of savings and credit cooperatives protect deposits by securing the solvency of the institution as a whole.
Gibraltar	22,614	20,000	0.75	Most	1	Coinsurance of 90 percent on all insured accounts.
Greece	22,614	20,000	1.43	Savings and checking accounts as well as foreign currency deposits are covered. Illegal deposits as well as negotiable CDs, acceptances, promissory notes, and repurchase agreements are excluded.	0	
Hungary	26,749	6,000,000	3.18	Hungary insures registered deposits. These include savings accounts, CDs, and foreign currency deposits.	0	Hungary insures registered deposits but excludes the deposits of the government, insiders, professional investors, and money launderers.
Iceland	22,614	20,000	0.63	Most. Savings accounts, checking accounts, CDs, traveler's checks, money orders, certified drafts of checks, and foreign currency deposits.	0	Coverage in Iceland in principle is full. Above the limit of €20,000, payment is in proportion to the resources of the fund.
Ireland	22,614	20,000	0.60	Ireland does not insure CDs.	1	The maximum amount payable to a depositor is 90 percent of the aggregate deposits held, subject to a maximum of €20,000.
Isle of Man	24,516	15,000	0.81	Most. Savings accounts, checking accounts, CDs, and foreign currency deposits.	1	Maximum compensation to any one depositor is the lower of £15,000 or 75 percent of amount deposited.
Italy	116,789	103,291	4.56	Italy insures all deposits except bearer deposits.	0	
Latvia	9,934	9,000	2.46	Deposits of natural persons, excluding illegal deposits.	0	The coverage limit will increase steadily to reach EU levels in 2008. In 2004 and 2005, the limit was LVL 6,000; in 2006 and 2007, LVL 9,000. From January 1, 2008, coverage in lats will be equivalent to €20,000.
Lithuania	16,370	45,000	3.11	Most, including savings accounts, CDs, money orders, and deposits in currencies of EU members or in U.S. dollars. Anonymous and illegal deposits are excluded.	10,000	Coinsurance of 90 percent above the basic coverage of LL 10,000 (from January 1, 2004). From January 1, 2007, the coverage limit will be LL 60,000; the coinsurance scheme remains (coinsurance of 90 percent above the threshold of LL 10,000). From January 1, 2008, coverage in litas will be equivalent to €20,000. Coinsurance of 90 percent will start above a threshold of €3,000.
Luxembourg	22,614	20,000	0.39	Cash deposits and claims arising out of investment transactions. Deposits for which the depositor has obtained financial advantages that contributed to the deterioration of the financial situation of the credit institution are also excluded.	1	In the statute of the newly created DIF, coinsurance was eliminated. Formerly, there was coinsurance of 90 percent.

Table A6 (continued)

Country	Coverage (In U.S. dollars)	Coverage Limit (Domestic currency)	Coverage Ratio of 2003 GDP Per Capita	Types of Deposits Eligible	Coinsurance (Above threshold of)[1]	Description
Macedonia, FYR	22,614	20,000	10.03	Current account and savings deposits, traveler's checks and money orders of resident natural persons in denars and foreign currencies. Deposits related to transactions used for money laundering are excluded.	10,000	Coverage is 100 percent for an amount of up to €10,000 in denar equivalent, and 90 percent for amounts between €10,000 and €20,000 in denar equivalent, but not exceeding €20,000 in denar equivalent.
Malta	22,614	8,000	2.25	Most	0	The amount of compensation is the lesser amount of 90 percent in respect to that depositor's eligible deposits or the Maltese equivalent of €20,000 calculated on the official rate prevailing on the date of settlement of the claim.
Netherlands	22,614	20,000	0.71	Deposits and investments.	0	
Norway	282,477	2,000,000	5.84	Most, including savings accounts, checking accounts, annuity contracts, CDs, and credit balances deriving from payment transfer orders or other ordinary banking services.	0	
Poland	25,440	22,500	4.71	Deposits and receivables resulting from other bank transactions, including savings accounts, checking accounts, CDs, money orders, and foreign currency deposits.	1	€1,000 paid in zlotys without coinsurance, then 90 percent coinsurance to €22,500.
Portugal	28,267	25,000	1.96	Portugal guarantees demand, time, and foreign currency deposits. High-rate deposits are excluded under certain circumstances.	0	
Romania	3,842	Indexed	1.58	The DIS in Romania protects household deposits (including foreign households) and excludes interbank, government, insider, and illegal deposits from coverage.	0	
Russia	3,264	100,000	1.08	Retail deposits of physical persons. Bearer bonds, deposits opened in connection with business activities, deposits placed in trustee management, and deposits paying exceptionally high interest are excluded.	0	
Serbia and Montenegro	86	5,000	0.03	. . .	0	
Slovak Republic	22,614	20,000	3.76	Most	1	Compensation is provided at 90 percent of the nominal value of deposits of one depositor in one bank. With the accession of the Slovak Republic to the European Union, compensation will be provided of up to €20,000, converted to Slovak koruny, whereby the system of deposit protection in the Slovak Republic would guarantee deposits in line with deposit protection rules of the European Union.
Slovenia	24,662	5,100,000	1.79	Most, including annuity contracts, CDs, and foreign currency deposits, but excluding bearer deposits.	0	

Table A6 *(concluded)*

Country	Coverage (In U.S. dollars)	Coverage Limit (Domestic currency)	Coverage Ratio of 2003 GDP Per Capita	Types of Deposits Eligible	Coinsurance (Above threshold of)[1]	Description
Spain	22,614	20,000	1.08	Most, including savings accounts, checking accounts, guaranteed investment certificates, and foreign currency deposits.	0	
Sweden	30,916	250,000	0.92	Officially, only nominal balances that are available to the depositor at short notice, including savings and checking accounts and foreign currency deposits.	0	
Switzerland	22,277	30,000	0.53	Savings deposits	0	
Turkey	33,429	50,000 million	9.35	Savings deposits made in local currency by natural persons and foreign exchange deposit accounts having the effect of savings deposit accounts opened by natural persons with branches in the country of banks operating in Turkey.	0	Turkey has implicitly provided unlimited coverage since May 1994. The full guarantee was made explicit in late 1999. It was rolled back in 2004.
Ukraine	281	1,500	0.27	Most	0	
United Kingdom	57,203	31,700	1.90	Most, including savings and checking accounts, foreign currency and term deposits.	1	Coverage is 100 percent of the first £2,000 and 90 percent of the next £33,000, so the value of total protected deposits is £35,000 and the maximum compensation is £317,000.
Middle East						
Algeria	389	30,000	0.19	. . .	1	. . .
Bahrain	5,641	15,000	0.46	All held in Bahraini offices of full commercial banks, except illegal ones.	1	Bahrain covers the lesser of 75 percent of a deposit or US$5,640, as long as the fund's total outlays do not exceed US$9.4 million. In this situation, coverage is determined on a pro rata basis.
Lebanon	3,317	5,000,000	0.67	Most. Lebanon insures all deposits denominated in Lebanese pounds, under a transitory law passed in 1991, which initially was due to expire at end-1998. Deposits denominated in foreign currency are also insured.	0	
Morocco	5,241	50,000	3.64	All	0	If the fund proves to be insufficient in Morocco, depositor compensation is reduced pro rata.
Oman	52,016	20,000	5.60	Most. Oman excludes interbank and illegal deposits.	1	Depositor is insured only for RO 20,000, subject to coinsurance of 75 percent of the net deposit value.

Sources: Country authorities; and IMF staff.
[1]Yes = 1; no = 0.

Table A7. Types of Deposits Covered and Excluded in Countries with Limited Explicit Deposits

Country	Type of Coverage[1]	Excludes Foreign Currencies[2]	Interbank Deposits[2]	Government Deposits[2]	Insider Deposits[2]	Illegal Deposits[2]	High-Rate Deposits[2]	Offsetting[2]
Africa								
Kenya	0	0	I	0	0	0	0	0
Nigeria	0	0	0	0	I	I	0	0
Sudan	...	I	I	...	...	...	...	...
Tanzania	2	0	0	0	0	0	0	0
Uganda	0	I	I	0	0	0	0	0
Zimbabwe	2	I	I	0	0	0	0	0
Americas								
Argentina	2	0	I	0	0	0	I	I
The Bahamas	2	0	0	0	0	0	0	0
Brazil	2	I	I	I	I	0	0	I
Canada	2	I	0	0	0	0	0	0
Chile	0	0	I	0	0	0	0	0
Colombia	2	0	I	0	0	0	0	I
Dominican Republic	0	0	I	0	0	0	0	0
Ecuador	0	0	0	0	I	0	I	0
El Salvador	2	0	I	0	I	I	0	0
Guatemala	2	0	0	0	I	I	0	0
Honduras	0	0	I	I	I	I	I	0
Jamaica	0	0	I	0	0	0	0	0
Mexico	2	0	I	0	I	I	0	I
Nicaragua	2	0	I	I	I	I	I	0
Paraguay	2	0	I	0	I	I	0	0
Peru	0	0	I	I	I	I	0	0
Trinidad and Tobago	2	I	I	0	0	0	0	0
United States	2	0	0	0	0	0	0	0
Venezuela	0	I	I	0	0	0	0	I
Asia								
Bangladesh	0	I	I	I	0	0	0	0
Hong Kong SAR	2	0	I	0	I	I	0	0
India	2	0	I	I	0	I	0	0
Indonesia	2	I	0	0	0	0	0	I
Japan	2	I	0	I	I	0	I	I
Kazakhstan	2	0	I	I	I	0	I	0
Korea	2	I	I	I	0	I	0	0
Marshall Islands	2	0	0	0	0	0	0	0
Micronesia	2	0	0	0	0	0	0	0
Philippines	2	0	0	0	0	I	0	0
Sri Lanka	0	I	I	I	0	0	0	0
Taiwan Province of China	2	I	I	I	0	0	0	0
Turkmenistan	...	0	I	...	...	...	...	...
Vietnam	2	I	0	0	0	0	0	0
Europe								
Albania	0	0	I	I	I	I	0	I
Austria	0	0	I	I	I	I	0	0
Belarus	2	0	I	I	I	0	I	I
Belgium	0	0	I	I	0	0	I	0
Bosnia and Herzegovina	2	0	0	I	I	I	I	I
Bulgaria	0	0	I	I	I	I	I	0
Croatia	2	0	I	I	I	0	0	...
Cyprus	2	I	I	I	I	I	0	0
Czech Rep.	2	I	I	0	I	I	0	0
Denmark	2	0	I	0	I	I	0	0

Table A7 *(concluded)*

Country	Type of Coverage[1]	Excludes Foreign Currencies[2]	Interbank Deposits[2]	Government Deposits[2]	Insider Deposits[2]	Illegal Deposits[2]	High-Rate Deposits[2]	Offsetting[2]
Estonia	2	0	I	I	I	I	I	0
Finland	2	0	I	I	I	I	0	0
France	2	0	I	I	I	I	I	I
Germany	2	0	I	I	I	I	I	0
Gibraltar	2	0	I	I	I	I	0	0
Greece	2	0	I	0	I	I	0	0
Hungary	2	0	I	I	I	I	I	0
Iceland	2	0	I	0	0	I	0	I
Ireland	2	0	I	I	I	I	0	0
Isle of Man	2	0	I	…	I	I	0	0
Italy	0	0	I	I	I	I	0	0
Latvia	0	0	I	I	I	I	0	I
Lithuania	2	0	I	0	I	I	0	0
Luxembourg	2	0	I	I	I	I	I	0
Macedonia, FYR	2	0	I	I	I	I	I	0
Malta	2	I	I	I	I	I	I	0
Netherlands	2	0	I	I	I	I	0	0
Norway	2	0	I	0	0	0	0	0
Poland	2	0	I	I	I	0	0	0
Portugal	0	0	I	I	I	I	I	0
Romania	0	0	I	I	I	0	0	I
Russia	0	0	I	I	I	I	I	…
Serbia and Montenegro	2	0	I	…	…	…	…	…
Slovak Republic	2	0	I	I	I	I	0	0
Slovenia	2	0	I	I	I	I	0	0
Spain	0	0	I	I	I	I	0	I
Sweden	2	0	I	0	0	0	0	I
Switzerland	0	I	I	I	0	0	0	0
Turkey	2	0	I	I	I	0	0	I
Ukraine	2	0	I	I	I	I	I	…
United Kingdom	2	0	I	I	I	I	0	0
Middle East								
Algeria	2	I	I	I	I	I	…	…
Bahrain	0	0	I	I	I	I	0	I
Jordan	2	I	I	I	0	I	0	0
Lebanon	2	0	I	0	I	0	0	I
Morocco	0	I	0	0	0	0	0	0
Oman	2	0	I	0	I	I	0	0

Sources: Country authorities; and IMF staff.

[1]Per depositor = 0; per institution = 1; per depositor per institution = 2; other = 3.

[2]Yes = 1; no = 0.

Table A8. Administering the Deposit Insurance System

Country	Administration[1]	Legally Separate Entity[2]	Governance Arrangements	Information Exchange
Africa				
Kenya	2	1	Independent de jure, but in practice is an integral part of the central bank, which is also the bank supervisor. The board shall consist of (1) the governor of the central bank as chair, (2) the treasury secretary, and (3) five members appointed by the ministry of finance in consultation with the central bank to represent the interest of institutions.	By law, the deposit insurance agency receives on- and off-site reports.
Nigeria	1	1	The deposit insurance agency is an independent agency with significant mandates. Relationship with the ministry of finance, which (together with the central bank) supervises it, is reported to be effective. The central bank is also the bank supervisor. The five-member board is appointed by the president of Nigeria and includes the governor of the central bank, the ministry of finance, plus the deposit insurance agency's managing director and two executive directors.	Yes, cooperation is good. The Nigerian Deposit Insurance Corporation conducts on- and off-site supervision.
Sudan	...	...		
Tanzania	1	1	The deposit insurance agency is independent, but relies on the central bank to provide staff, resources, and supervisory functions. The board consists of the governor of the central bank as the chair, two representatives from the treasury, and three other members appointed by the ministry of finance.	The deposit insurance agency is hosted within the central bank, which is also the bank supervisor. However, information exchange is limited.
Uganda	1	0	No separate deposit insurance agency; the deposit insurance system is responsibility of the central bank, which is also the bank supervisor.	Because the deposit insurance system is administered by the central bank, access to information is given.
Zimbabwe	1	1	Although the central bank is still involved in many operations, the deposit insurance agency is set up as a separate legal entity. 50 percent of the board of directors are representatives from the central bank, 50 percent come from contributing institutions. In a second phase, the Deposit Protection Board should have broader independence and responsibilities.	There is a memorandum of understanding (MOU) between the deposit insurance agency and the central bank. The deposit insurance agency receives data on deposits electronically from the insured banks and the central bank, which is the bank supervisor. According to country authorities, there is still scope for improvement concerning cooperation.
America				
Argentina	2	1	The deposit insurance agency is a private legal entity that is authorized by the central bank, led by central bank representatives. It cooperates with banking supervisors.	Superintendency division of the central bank performs examinations; the deposit insurance system receives information specified ex ante, formal and informal arrangements to share information. Officially, the deposit insurance system is consulted when the central bank enters into agreements with intermediaries.

Table A8 *(continued)*

Country	Administration[1]	Legally Separate Entity[2]	Governance Arrangements	Information Exchange
The Bahamas	I	I	The deposit insurance agency is a separate corporation subordinated to the central bank and the ministry of finance. Board of management appointed by the ministry of finance. The board of management consists of the central bank governor, two other central bank representatives, the financial secretary, and two other persons. Deposit insurance system shall act only on advice of the central bank.	By law, the deposit insurance system receives data from member banks and the central bank. The deposit insurance system is run by central bank employees.
Brazil	3	I	Insurance is provided by private nonprofit company supervised by the central bank. All five board members are bank managers.	The deposit insurance agency should receive necessary information from the central bank, but there are no legal provisions or arrangements for information exchange.
Canada	I	I	Members of the independent board include, ex officio, one member each from the central bank and the ministry of finance, and two from the banking supervisor. The deposit insurance agency is accountable to parliament through the ministry of finance.	Yes, good—facilitated by a Strategic Alliance Agreement between the deposit insurance agency and the banking supervisor.
Chile	I	0	No separate deposit insurance agency. The central bank protects demand deposits; the ministry of finance, savings deposits. Deposit insurance system is run by the central bank, which is closely related to the banking supervisor.	Significant exchanges of information among the central bank, banking supervisor, and ministry of finance.
Colombia	I	I	The composition of the board of directors is as follows: minister of finance, central bank governor, superintendent of securities, and two members appointed by the president (one of them from the financial sector). The superintendent of banks participates without a voting right.	Agreement for sharing information in place. The deposit insurance agency is dependent on superintendent of banks to receive information.
Dominican Republic	I	0	The central bank establishes and administers the fund.	The central bank administers the fund and has access to supervisory information through the bank supervisor.
Ecuador	I	I	The deposit insurance agency is an autonomous, public-law institution under the bank supervisor. The four-member board includes one representative each from the banking supervisor, the ministry of finance, the central bank, and the public.	Information is obtained from the banking supervisor.
El Salvador	I	I	The deposit insurance agency is an autonomous public institution, subject to oversight by the bank supervisor. It consults with the central bank, the ministry of finance, and the banking supervisor on bank rehabilitation. Two of the five board members come from the central bank and two from healthy banks.	By law it obtains the information it needs from the central bank and the banking supervisor.

Table A8 (continued)

Country	Administration[1]	Legally Separate Entity[2]	Governance Arrangements	Information Exchange
Guatemala	1	0	The deposit insurance system is supervised by the bank supervisor. The Bank of Guatemala, the central bank, is the trustee of the deposit insurance system funds, and represents it before the monetary board.	The deposit insurance system obtains data from the banks each month to calculate premiums, and from the bank supervisor when it needs extra funds.
Honduras	1	1	The deposit insurance system is a decentralized entity under the central bank, but has technical, administrative, and budgetary independence. Three of its five board members are public officials, two are private, including one from the bankers' association.	By law the bank supervisor and central bank are required to provide data requested by the Deposit Insurance Fund (Fondo de Seguro de Depósitos), which can also obtain data from member banks.
Jamaica	1	1	The deposit insurance agency is an independent statutory body that cooperates with the central bank, which is also the bank supervisor. It needs the approval of the ministry of finance. Of the seven board members, three come ex officio from the government and four are appointed by the ministry of finance.	Yes, sharing is required by law, but has proved problematic in practice, because the Jamaica Deposit Insurance Corporation must request on-site reports from the bank supervisor.
Mexico	1	1	The deposit insurance agency (IPAB) has legal and financial independence. Its seven-member governing board is composed of three ex officio members (the heads of the central bank, ministry of finance, and bank supervisor) and four congressionally approved independent members.	Yes, by law, but IPAB is dependent on the bank supervisor and the banks for data. The deposit insurance agency can participate or solicit an on-site inspection of a member institution if it has provided financial assistance to the institution.
Nicaragua	1	1	The deposit insurance system is legally independent, but hosted within the central bank, which lends staff and resources. It is run by a board of directors, consisting of the central bank governor, the superintendent of banks, the minister of finance, a representative appointed by the president of the republic, and one representative of financial institutions.	
Paraguay	1	0	The central bank, which is also the bank supervisor, manages and administers the deposit insurance system.	Because the deposit insurance system is administered by the central bank, which is also the bank supervisor, access to information is given.
Peru	2	1	The deposit insurance agency is a private legal entity that is subject to regulation by the bank supervisor. Of its six board members, one comes from the central bank, one from the bank supervisor, one from the ministry of finance, and the other three are drawn from financial institutions, appointed by the member assembly. The majority of dedicated staff comes from the bank supervisor.	The bank supervisor determines premiums, effects reimbursement, and makes the payments, after having demanded funds from the deposit insurance system. As a consequence, information exchange is limited and there is no formal arrangement between safety net players.

Table A8 *(continued)*

Country	Administration[1]	Legally Separate Entity[2]	Governance Arrangements	Information Exchange
Trinidad and Tobago	1	1	The deposit insurance agency is a separate, independent legal entity, but the central bank and ministry of finance set the bylaws. The deposit insurance agency is housed in the central bank.	Information exchange only at the discretion of the central bank.
United States	1	1	FDIC board members are appointed by the president of the United States and must be confirmed by the U.S. Senate. Three of the five members are FDIC board members (including a chair and vice chair); the other two members serve by virtue of their positions as heads of the office of the comptroller of the currency and office of thrift supervision, both bureaus of the treasury department.	Yes, but disagreements leading to delays have occurred between the different agencies involved. The deposit insurance agency has backup supervisory authority for those banks it does not supervise, but rarely uses it.
Venezuela	1	1	The deposit insurance agency is an autonomous legal entity that is supervised by the bank supervisor (and the ministry of finance for administrative purposes). The board has six members: the chair and four others are appointed by the president. It also includes one representative from the banks, one from the labor union, and one from the insurance agency's employees.	By law, the deposit insurance system obtains the examination reports of weak banks and information on deposits to calculate premiums from the bank supervisor.
Asia				
Bangladesh	1	1	Trustee board for operation and administration. By law, the board of directors of Bangladesh Bank shall be the trustee board of the fund.	Data for payout comes from liquidator.
Hong Kong SAR	2	1	The deposit insurance board should comprise not less than 7 but not more than 10 members. Two members are ex officio (from among the secretary for financial services, the monetary authority, the Chief Executive Officer (CEO) of the board), and up to seven are lay members. Lay members will have a majority over ex officio and executive members to ensure sufficient independence.	In certain circumstances, the Hong Kong Monetary Authority could collect information on behalf of the deposit insurance system.
India	1	1	The deposit insurance agency is a wholly owned subsidiary of the central bank, of which the bank supervisor is also a part. There are no supervisors on the deposit insurance system board.	The deposit insurance system has access to bank records by law and depends on the bank supervisor for exam reports. Needs improvement.
Indonesia	1	1	The Indonesian Deposit Insurance Corporation (IDIC) is an independent agency with a six-person board of commissioners (one from the ministry of finance, one from the central bank, one from the Bank Supervision Department, and three from outside).	A separate "note of agreement" provides for exchange of information between the IDIC and the bank supervisors.

Table A8 *(continued)*

Country	Administration[1]	Legally Separate Entity[2]	Governance Arrangements	Information Exchange
Japan	2	I	The board is composed of members of executive management of Deposit Insurance Corporation of Japan and external persons that are appointed by the governor with approval of the prime minister and the minister of finance. The deposit insurance system is supervised by the Financial Services Agency and the ministry of finance.	The law authorizes the deposit insurance system to request information from the government and the central bank.
Kazakhstan	2	I	The deposit insurance system is a separate legal entity. The central bank appoints three of nine directors and the ministry of finance appoints one other.	Yes, on condition and deposits by agreement with the central bank and from members.
Korea	I	I	The KDIC reports to the ministry of finance and is separate from the central bank and the bank supervisor. It is run by a board of directors and a policy committee. The president of the committee is appointed by the president of the republic. Members of the committee include representatives of various ministries, the Financial Supervisory Commission, and the Bank of Korea.	The KDIC collects the data it needs on deposits and bank condition. Also, the deposit insurance agency can require the bank supervisor to examine member banks.
Marshall Islands	I	I	As in the United States.	As in the United States.
Micronesia	I	I	There is no relationship between the local supervisors and the U.S. FDIC, which insures the banks.	There are no arrangements for sharing information.
Philippines	I	I	The deposit insurance agency is separate and independent and has played a major role in recent bank restructuring efforts. The board is composed of five members, with three ex officio members, namely: secretary of finance, Philippine Deposit Insurance Corporation president, and central bank governor. Two part-time members from the private sector are appointed by the president of the Philippines to serve on the board for six years.	Relies on the central bank and bank supervisor for exam reports. The right to perform on-site examinations was repealed in 2000. An information exchange agreement between the central bank and the deposit insurance agency was signed in 2002, but information exchange is still not fully implemented.
Sri Lanka	I	0	The deposit insurance system is administered by the supervision department of the central bank.	Because the deposit insurance system is part of the supervision department of the central bank, direct access to information is given.
Taiwan Province of China	I	I	The deposit insurance agency was established by the ministry of finance, but its role has grown subsequently. It has, for example, taken over responsibility for examining institutions from the ministry of finance.	Yes, the deposit insurance agency is the bank supervisor and conducts bank examinations.
Turkmenistan	I	...	...	...

Table A8 *(continued)*

Country	Administration[1]	Legally Separate Entity[2]	Governance Arrangements	Information Exchange
Vietnam	1	1	Legally independent.	Information exchange between the deposit insurance agency and bank supervisor is stipulated in the legislation. The deposit insurance agency also has the authority to inspect banks.
Europe				
Albania	1	1	The agency is a public legal institution and shall have operational and financial autonomy from any other entity. The agency prepares an annual report approved by the supervisory authority and submits it to the parliament and to the council of ministers.	There is an MOU between the deposit insurance agency and the central bank. The deposit insurance agency receives data from the insured banks and the central bank, which is the bank supervisor. Periodically informs the Bank of Albania and the insured banks about the insurance deposit policies, the financial situation of the banks, and its budget.
Austria	3	1	There are multiple schemes privately managed by the respective bankers' associations.	There are detailed provisions on risk assessment and cooperation in the law.
Belarus	1	0	The guarantee fund is administered by the central bank.	The deposit insurance system is hosted within the central bank, which, as bank supervisor, has access to all relevant information.
Belgium	2	1	The deposit insurance system has the responsibility of a separate banking supervisor that may be transferred to the central bank.	Sharing is authorized.
Bosnia and Herzegovina	1	1	The two-member governing body is selected by parliament. The five-member management board includes, ex officio, the director of the banking agency and the minister of finance. The remaining members are financial and banking experts appointed by the president of the federation, upon proposal of the government.	
Bulgaria	2	1	The deposit insurance agency is a separate legal entity, but dependent on the central bank. Five-member board— one from government, one central bank, one bank, and two independent.	The deposit insurance agency is dependent on the central bank to provide information on condition. The deposit insurance agency can demand information from member banks.
Croatia	1	1	The deposit insurance agency is part of the Bank Restructuring Agency, which is independent de jure. Government officials are members of the deposit insurance agency board.	Yes, informally, as needed. Members are required, by law, to provide data to the deposit insurance agency on deposits and condition.

Table A8 (continued)

Country	Administration[1]	Legally Separate Entity[2]	Governance Arrangements	Information Exchange
Cyprus	1	1	Though a separate legal entity, the deposit insurance system is hosted within the central bank. The chair and vice-chair of the management committee are, ex officio, the governor of the central bank and the head of banking supervision. Three additional members are appointed by the central bank, two of them nominated by the association of banks and one by the ministry of finance.	Because the central bank administers the deposit insurance system and the central bank is the banking supervisor, access to information is given.
Czech Republic	1	1	The deposit insurance agency is a separate legal entity. Its board members are appointed by the ministry of finance. One of the five board members is from the central bank and two are from the banks.	No formal arrangement to exchange information, but it is obtained from depositors and the central bank.
Denmark	3	1	The private, independent deposit insurance agency is under the supervision of the banking supervisor, but is located in the central bank, which provides staff. Though privately run, the board is appointed by the minister of economic affairs. Six members of the board come from member institutions; two represent depositors and investors.	Yes, the changed law requires close cooperation between the deposit insurance agency and the bank supervisor.
Estonia	2	1	The deposit insurance agency was recently reorganized, and now is jointly responsible for different protection schemes. The supervisory board consists of eight members who have been appointed by parliament, government, central bank, financial supervision authority, banking association, and by the organizations representing the investment institutions and pension management companies. The term of authority of the supervisory board of the guarantee fund is four years.	Yes, as required by the law, the central bank and member banks provide data. Information for a payout comes from the liquidator.
Finland	3	1	The deposit insurance agency is supervised by the banking supervisor and the ministry of finance; the central bank has no role.	The government sets the standards for corporation.
France	3	1	The new deposit insurance system board is private and independent and represents its member institutions. It always has representatives from its four largest contributors. The banking supervisor sets the premiums.	Yes, by law, but it is difficult in practice. Banking supervisor assesses risks, calculates the risk adjustment, and passes the data to the deposit insurance agency.

Table A8 *(continued)*

Country	Administration[1]	Legally Separate Entity[2]	Governance Arrangements	Information Exchange
Germany	3 (2)	1	The official scheme is run by the bankers' association and supervised by the banking supervisor, which also determines compensation and other important details. The ministry of finance approves the bylaws and sets premiums. The central bank is not involved. The private scheme is run by a commission of 10 persons that represent groups of commercial banks. It has no public oversight. It cooperates with the banking supervisor.	The deposit insurance agency can collect information, which it must share with the banking supervisor by law. It is also obliged to consult the banking supervisor.
Gibraltar	2	1	The deposit insurance agency is independent de jure. The ministry of industry and trade appoints the six-member board from among the banking supervisor, auditors, lawyers, and bankers.	Banks provide data for calculating premiums; depositors and the liquidator for payouts.
Greece	2	1	The deposit insurance agency is a legal entity governed by private law. It is run by the bankers' association, which has full decision-making powers, under the budgetary supervision of the minister of the economy. Its seven-member board is appointed by the ministry of finance, the central bank, and the bankers' association.	Members have to report data regularly. The deposit insurance agency has no power to inspect banks. Data come from the banking supervisor for premiums (not condition), the failed bank for payouts, and the home supervisor for foreign branches.
Hungary	2	1	The deposit insurance agency is a legal entity, separate from the bank supervisor and central bank, but the state grants it limited authority. The board is appointed from the ministry of finance, central bank, bank supervisor, the CEO, and the banking industry.	Yes, by formal agreement, with the bank supervisor and from members.
Iceland	2	1	One-third of the directors are appointed by the minister of commerce, one-third by the commercial banks, one-sixth by the savings banks, and one-sixth by the securities houses. There is one observer from the association of depositors and investors. The deposit insurance system is supervised by the bank supervisor.	Data come primarily from the banks and from an informal exchange with the bank supervisor.
Ireland	1	0	The deposit insurance system is run by the central bank.	. . .
Isle of Man	1	1	The scheme is administered by the scheme manager and the Financial Supervision Commission. The board of the Financial Supervision Commission effectively acts as the board of the scheme.	Because the bank supervisor administers the deposit insurance system, access to information is given.

Table A8 *(continued)*

Country	Administration[1]	Legally Separate Entity[2]	Governance Arrangements	Information Exchange
Italy	3	1	The private-consortium deposit insurance system is closely knit with the Bank of Italy (BOI), which is also the bank supervisor. The BOI approves the deposit insurance system bylaws. Although the scheme is privately run, all decisions must be approved by the central bank so the deposit insurance system has little independent authority.	Yes, by law, but formal notification is required and the issue is sensitive because the deposit insurance system is privately run. The deposit insurance system also obtains data directly from member banks.
Latvia	1	0	In 2001, the administration and management of the deposit insurance system was transferred to the newly created Financial Services Authority, the FCMC. The latter is accountable to the ministry of finance.	Because the deposit insurance system is managed by the FCMC, it has access to all relevant information.
Lithuania	1	1	The deposit insurance agency, an independent state enterprise, was established by and reports to the ministry of finance. Two of the five board members come from the central bank, and three from the ministry of finance.	By law, information is obtained directly from the banks and from the central bank.
Luxembourg	3	1	The deposit insurance agency is administered by a board of directors elected by the general meeting of all institutions participating in the scheme.	. . .
Macedonia, FYR	1	1	The managing board consists of five members appointed by the government: three proposed by the ministry of finance, one by the governor of the central bank, and one by the banking and insurance association. Members are appointed for a four-year term. The managing board reports to the government of Macedonia, FYR, for its operations.	Even though required by law, information exchange is said to be problematic. However, the deposit insurance agency was reorganized recently and is now administered by representatives of the central bank and the ministry of finance.
Malta	2	1	The management committee includes officials from the bank supervisor, the central bank, and the associations representing banks and investment services intermediaries, and a consumer representative. Although it is supposed to be independent from the government, most important decisions have to be taken in accordance with the bank supervisor.	Information exchange is established by law. The management committee has the right to request that participants, either directly or through the competent authority, submit data and information in the form it requests relevant for the proper administration of the scheme.
Netherlands	1	0	The deposit insurance system is run by the central bank.	The deposit insurance system, being run by the central bank, obtains data directly from the banks.

Table A8 *(continued)*

Country	Administration[1]	Legally Separate Entity[2]	Governance Arrangements	Information Exchange
Norway	3	1	The central bank and bank supervisor are represented on the deposit insurance agency boards, so each scheme has two public members on its seven-member board—one from the central bank and the other from the Banking and Securities Commission.	Yes, the law requires the central bank to provide requested data.
Poland	1	1	The fund is managed by the fund management board and administered by the fund council. The members of the latter are appointed and removed by the prime minister on mutual recommendation of the ministry of finance and central bank.	Yes, by law the central bank must supply the information the deposit insurance agency requests. It also obtains data from banks for its early detection system.
Portugal	1	1	The deposit insurance agency is an autonomous public legal entity housed at the central bank and is under ministry of finance direction.	The deposit insurance system obtains deposit and condition data directly from member banks, partly because it is hosted within the central bank, which is also the bank supervisor. By law, the central bank provides "technical and administrative services."
Romania	2	1	The deposit insurance agency is independent de jure, but the central bank, which is also the bank supervisor, approves its bylaws. Three of the seven board members are appointed by the central bank, and one each by the ministry of justice, the ministry of finance, and the bankers' association.	Yes
Russia	1	1	The deposit insurance system is to be administered by a new agency. The deposit insurance agency is to be a state corporation, independent of, but working closely with, the central bank. Its board of directors will consist of representatives of the government and the central bank. The central bank will play a crucial role in the administration of the scheme, because banks will be allowed to join it only with approval of the Central Bank of Russia.	. . .
Serbia and Montenegro	1	1	The governing body of the deposit insurance agency is a council made up of seven members appointed by the government. It is accountable to the government and provides annual reports to the parliament, the central bank, and the ministry of finance.	. . .

Table A8 *(continued)*

Country	Administration[1]	Legally Separate Entity[2]	Governance Arrangements	Information Exchange
Slovak Republic	2	I	The deposit insurance agency is independent de jure, but is supervised by the central bank. The board is composed of seven members: three (originally five) are elected and recalled by bank representatives, two (originally one) are representatives of the central bank, and two are representatives of the ministry of finance.	. . .
Slovenia	I	0	The deposit insurance system is administered and managed by the supervisory department of the central bank.	The deposit insurance system is hosted within the central bank, which, as bank supervisor, has access to all relevant information.
Spain	2	I	The deposit insurance agencies have public legal status under the central bank. They are administered by a management committee comprising eight members appointed by the minister of the economy, four representing the central bank, and the others representing credit institutions. The deputy governor of the central bank is the chair of each of the funds.	The deposit insurance system is entitled by law to demand all the information needed to carry out its function. Moreover, the composition of the governing bodies assures the coordination and sharing of information concerning member institutions.
Sweden	I	I	The deposit insurance agency is accountable to the ministry of finance; it consults with the bank supervisor and shares its premises. The managing board itself consists of seven members, all appointed by the government and comprising two politicians, one lawyer, three economists, and the chair, who is also a lawyer. The industry is not represented on the board.	Yes, but data come primarily from member institutions and the liquidator of a failed bank.
Switzerland	3	I	The deposit insurance system is run by the Swiss Bankers' Association. The banking commission is separate from the central bank.	Data are passed from banks to the bank supervisor, which conveys them to the deposit insurance system.
Turkey	I	I	The deposit insurance agency is a judicial entity under the newly independent bank supervisor.	Yes, the deposit insurance agency can request the data it needs from the parent bank supervisor.
Ukraine	I	I	The deposit insurance agency is an independent, state-run commercial organization, operated by the central bank. Two of its five board members come from the cabinet, two from the central bank, and one is a banker.	Yes, by law the deposit insurance agency obtains information from the central bank. It can also inspect banks. Data for payouts come from the liquidator.

Table A8 *(concluded)*

Country	Administration[1]	Legally Separate Entity[2]	Governance Arrangements	Information Exchange
United Kingdom	1	1	The deposit insurance agency acts as a separate legal entity with its own staff (previously, staff came from the bank supervisor and the central bank). However, the deposit insurance agency outsources many of its tasks to the Financial Services Authority (FSA), which also sets most of the bylaws. The members of the board of directors are appointed by the bank supervisor (FSA) and are not representative of member institutions.	The deposit insurance agency and the bank supervisor share information on the basis of an MOU. Information exchange is said to work properly.
Middle East				
Algeria	2	0	The deposit insurance agency is hosted within the central bank.	The deposit insurance agency is hosted within the central bank.
Bahrain	2	1	Of the 10 board members, 2 come from the central bank, 3 from various ministries, 1 from the chamber of commerce, and 4 from commercial banks. The final member is a liquidator.	Data for payout directly obtained from depositors.
Jordan	1	1	The deposit insurance system is governed by a board of directors, consisting of the governor of the central bank as the chair of the board, one of the governor's deputies, representatives from the ministry of finance and from the ministry of industry and trade, and two members appointed by the council of ministers based on the governor's recommendation.	The corporation is working currently with the central bank (bank's regulator, supervisor, and lender of last resort) to develop a memorandum of understanding. Initial draft was produced and currently under consideration.
Lebanon	2	1	The deposit insurance system is a cooperative, joint-stock company. Of its seven board members, three come from the government and four from the banks.	There is a bank secrecy law. Depositors submit claims to a court-appointed receivership committee, which conveys the data to the deposit insurance system.
Morocco	1	0	The deposit insurance system is administered by the central bank, which is also the bank supervisor. The ministry of finance promulgates the deposit insurance system regulations.	Nothing is stipulated in the law, but the bank supervisor and deposit insurance system are part of the same agency.
Oman	1	0	The deposit insurance agency is part of the central bank, but has separate accounts. The central bank can amend any rule governing the deposit insurance system at its discretion.	The central bank, which is also the bank supervisor, has the data it needs to operate the deposit insurance system.

Sources: Country authorities; and IMF staff.
[1]Official = 1; joint = 2; private = 3.
[2]Yes = 1; no = 0.

References

Canadian Deposit Insurance Corporation (CDIC), 2002. Available via the Internet: http://www.cdic.ca.

Cull, R., L.W. Senbet, and M. Sorge, 2006, "Deposit Insurance and Financial Development," *Journal of Money, Credit and Banking,* forthcoming.

Demirgüç-Kunt, Asli, and Enrica Detragiache, 2002, "Does Deposit Insurance Increase Banking System Stability? An Empirical Investigation," *Journal of Monetary Economics*, Vol. 49, No. 7, pp. 1373–406.

Demirgüç-Kunt, Asli, and Harry Huizinga, 2004, "Market Discipline and Deposit Insurance," *Journal of Monetary Economics*, Vol. 51, No. 2, pp. 375–99.

Demirgüç-Kunt, Asli, and Edward J. Kane, 2002, "Deposit Insurance Around the Globe: Where Does It Work?" *Journal of Economic Perspectives,* Vol. 16 (Spring), pp. 175–95.

Dewatripont, Mathias, and Jean Tirole, 1994, *The Prudential Regulation of Banks* (Cambridge, Massachusetts: MIT Press).

Diamond, Douglas W., and Philip H. Dybvig, 1983, "Bank Runs, Deposit Insurance, and Liquidity," *Journal of Political Economy*, Vol. 91 (June), pp. 401–19.

Eichengreen, Barry, and Carlos Arteta, 2000, "Banking Crises in Emerging Markets: Presumptions and Evidence," CIDER Working Paper C00–115 (Berkeley, California: Center for International and Development Economics Research, University of California at Berkeley).

Financial Stability Forum (FSF), 2001, "Guidance for Developing Effective Deposit Insurance Systems" (Basel: Bank for International Settlements).

Flannery, Mark A., 1998, "Using Market Information in Prudential Bank Supervision: A Review of the U.S. Empirical Evidence," *Journal of Money, Credit and Banking*, Vol. 30 (August).

Garcia, Gillian G.H., 1996, "Deposit Insurance: Obtaining the Benefits and Avoiding the Pitfalls," IMF Working Paper 96/83 (Washington: International Monetary Fund).

———, 1999, "Deposit Insurance: A Survey of Actual and Best Practices," IMF Working Paper 99/54 (Washington: International Monetary Fund).

———, 2000, Deposit Insurance: Actual and Good Practices, IMF Occasional Paper No. 197 (Washington: International Monetary Fund).

Gropp, Reint, and Jukka Vesala, 2004, "Deposit Insurance, Moral Hazard and Market Monitoring," ECB Working Paper No. 302 (Frankfurt: European Central Bank).

International Association of Deposit Insurers, 2003. Available via the Internet: http://www.iadi.org.

Kyei, Alexander, 1995, "Deposit Protection Arrangements: A Survey," IMF Working Paper 95/134 (Washington: International Monetary Fund).

Martinez Peria, Maria Soledad, and Sergio L. Schmukler, 2001, "Do Depositors Punish Banks for Bad Behavior? Market Discipline, Deposit Insurance, and Banking Crises," *Journal of Finance*, Vol. 56 (June), pp. 1029–51.

Recent Occasional Papers of the International Monetary Fund

251. The Design and Implementation of Deposit Insurance Systems, by David S. Hoelscher, Michael Taylor, and Ulrich H. Klueh. 2006.

250. Designing Monetary and Fiscal Policy in Low-Income Countries, by Abebe Aemro Selassie, Benedict Clements, Shamsuddin Tareq, Jan Kees Martijn, and Gabriel Di Bella. 2006.

249. Official Foreign Exchange Intervention, by Shogo Ishi, Jorge Iván Canales-Kriljenko, Roberto Guimarães, and Cem Karacadag. 2006.

248. Labor Market Performance in Transition: The Experience of Central and Eastern European Countries, by Jerald Schiff, Philippe Egoumé-Bossogo, Miho Ihara, Tetsuya Konuki, and Kornélia Krajnyák. 2006.

247. Rebuilding Fiscal Institutions in Post-Conflict Countries, by Sanjeev Gupta, Shamsuddin Tareq, Benedict Clements, Alex Segura-Ubiergo, Rina Bhattacharya, and Todd Mattina. 2005.

246. Experience with Large Fiscal Adjustments, by George C. Tsibouris, Mark A. Horton, Mark J. Flanagan, and Wojciech S. Maliszewski. 2005.

245. Budget System Reform in Emerging Economies: The Challenges and the Reform Agenda, by Jack Diamond. 2005.

244. Monetary Policy Implementation at Different Stages of Market Development, by a staff team led by Bernard J. Laurens. 2005.

243. Central America: Global Integration and Regional Cooperation, edited by Markus Rodlauer and Alfred Schipke. 2005.

242. Turkey at the Crossroads: From Crisis Resolution to EU Accession, by a staff team led by Reza Moghadam. 2005.

241. The Design of IMF-Supported Programs, by Atish Ghosh, Charis Christofides, Jun Kim, Laura Papi, Uma Ramakrishnan, Alun Thomas, and Juan Zalduendo. 2005.

240. Debt-Related Vulnerabilities and Financial Crises: An Application of the Balance Sheet Approach to Emerging Market Countries, by Christoph Rosenberg, Ioannis Halikias, Brett House, Christian Keller, Jens Nystedt, Alexander Pitt, and Brad Setser. 2005.

239. GEM: A New International Macroeconomic Model, by Tamim Bayoumi, with assistance from Douglas Laxton, Hamid Faruqee, Benjamin Hunt, Philippe Karam, Jaewoo Lee, Alessandro Rebucci, and Ivan Tchakarov. 2004.

238. Stabilization and Reforms in Latin America: A Macroeconomic Perspective on the Experience Since the Early 1990s, by Anoop Singh, Agnès Belaisch, Charles Collyns, Paula De Masi, Reva Krieger, Guy Meredith, and Robert Rennhack. 2005.

237. Sovereign Debt Structure for Crisis Prevention, by Eduardo Borensztein, Marcos Chamon, Olivier Jeanne, Paolo Mauro, and Jeromin Zettelmeyer. 2004.

236. Lessons from the Crisis in Argentina, by Christina Daseking, Atish R. Ghosh, Alun Thomas, and Timothy Lane. 2004.

235. A New Look at Exchange Rate Volatility and Trade Flows, by Peter B. Clark, Natalia Tamirisa, and Shang-Jin Wei, with Azim Sadikov and Li Zeng. 2004.

234. Adopting the Euro in Central Europe: Challenges of the Next Step in European Integration, by Susan M. Schadler, Paulo F. Drummond, Louis Kuijs, Zuzana Murgasova, and Rachel N. van Elkan. 2004.

233. Germany's Three-Pillar Banking System: Cross-Country Perspectives in Europe, by Allan Brunner, Jörg Decressin, Daniel Hardy, and Beata Kudela. 2004.

232. China's Growth and Integration into the World Economy: Prospects and Challenges, edited by Eswar Prasad. 2004.

231. Chile: Policies and Institutions Underpinning Stability and Growth, by Eliot Kalter, Steven Phillips, Marco A. Espinosa-Vega, Rodolfo Luzio, Mauricio Villafuerte, and Manmohan Singh. 2004.

230. Financial Stability in Dollarized Countries, by Anne-Marie Gulde, David Hoelscher, Alain Ize, David Marston, and Gianni De Nicoló. 2004.

229. Evolution and Performance of Exchange Rate Regimes, by Kenneth S. Rogoff, Aasim M. Husain, Ashoka Mody, Robin Brooks, and Nienke Oomes. 2004.

228. Capital Markets and Financial Intermediation in The Baltics, by Alfred Schipke, Christian Beddies, Susan M. George, and Niamh Sheridan. 2004.

227. U.S. Fiscal Policies and Priorities for Long-Run Sustainability, edited by Martin Mühleisen and Christopher Towe. 2004.

226. Hong Kong SAR: Meeting the Challenges of Integration with the Mainland, edited by Eswar Prasad, with contributions from Jorge Chan-Lau, Dora Iakova, William Lee, Hong Liang, Ida Liu, Papa N'Diaye, and Tao Wang. 2004.

225. Rules-Based Fiscal Policy in France, Germany, Italy, and Spain, by Teresa Dában, Enrica Detragiache, Gabriel di Bella, Gian Maria Milesi-Ferretti, and Steven Symansky. 2003.

224. Managing Systemic Banking Crises, by a staff team led by David S. Hoelscher and Marc Quintyn. 2003.

223. Monetary Union Among Member Countries of the Gulf Cooperation Council, by a staff team led by Ugo Fasano. 2003.

222. Informal Funds Transfer Systems: An Analysis of the Informal Hawala System, by Mohammed El Qorchi, Samuel Munzele Maimbo, and John F. Wilson. 2003.

221. Deflation: Determinants, Risks, and Policy Options, by Manmohan S. Kumar. 2003.

220. Effects of Financial Globalization on Developing Countries: Some Empirical Evidence, by Eswar S. Prasad, Kenneth Rogoff, Shang-Jin Wei, and Ayhan Kose. 2003.

219. Economic Policy in a Highly Dollarized Economy: The Case of Cambodia, by Mario de Zamaroczy and Sopanha Sa. 2003.

218. Fiscal Vulnerability and Financial Crises in Emerging Market Economies, by Richard Hemming, Michael Kell, and Axel Schimmelpfennig. 2003.

217. Managing Financial Crises: Recent Experience and Lessons for Latin America, edited by Charles Collyns and G. Russell Kincaid. 2003.

216. Is the PRGF Living Up to Expectations? An Assessment of Program Design, by Sanjeev Gupta, Mark Plant, Benedict Clements, Thomas Dorsey, Emanuele Baldacci, Gabriela Inchauste, Shamsuddin Tareq, and Nita Thacker. 2002.

215. Improving Large Taxpayers' Compliance: A Review of Country Experience, by Katherine Baer. 2002.

214. Advanced Country Experiences with Capital Account Liberalization, by Age Bakker and Bryan Chapple. 2002.

213. The Baltic Countries: Medium-Term Fiscal Issues Related to EU and NATO Accession, by Johannes Mueller, Christian Beddies, Robert Burgess, Vitali Kramarenko, and Joannes Mongardini. 2002.

212. Financial Soundness Indicators: Analytical Aspects and Country Practices, by V. Sundararajan, Charles Enoch, Armida San José, Paul Hilbers, Russell Krueger, Marina Moretti, and Graham Slack. 2002.

211. Capital Account Liberalization and Financial Sector Stability, by a staff team led by Shogo Ishii and Karl Habermeier. 2002.

210. IMF-Supported Programs in Capital Account Crises, by Atish Ghosh, Timothy Lane, Marianne Schulze-Ghattas, Aleš Bulíř, Javier Hamann, and Alex Mourmouras. 2002.

209. Methodology for Current Account and Exchange Rate Assessments, by Peter Isard, Hamid Faruqee, G. Russell Kincaid, and Martin Fetherston. 2001.

208. Yemen in the 1990s: From Unification to Economic Reform, by Klaus Enders, Sherwyn Williams, Nada Choueiri, Yuri Sobolev, and Jan Walliser. 2001.

207. Malaysia: From Crisis to Recovery, by Kanitta Meesook, Il Houng Lee, Olin Liu, Yougesh Khatri, Natalia Tamirisa, Michael Moore, and Mark H. Krysl. 2001.

206. The Dominican Republic: Stabilization, Structural Reform, and Economic Growth, by a staff team led by Philip Young comprising Alessandro Giustiniani, Werner C. Keller, and Randa E. Sab and others. 2001.

205. Stabilization and Savings Funds for Nonrenewable Resources, by Jeffrey Davis, Rolando Ossowski, James Daniel, and Steven Barnett. 2001.

Note: For information on the titles and availability of Occasional Papers not listed, please consult the IMF's *Publications Catalog* or contact IMF Publication Services.